Attention Grabbing Tools for involving parents in their children's learning

JANE BASKWILL

Pembroke Publishers Limited

With thanks to David Doake and Eric Smith, mentors and friends who started me on this journey, and all the parents and teachers over the years who have helped inform my work.

© 2013 Pembroke Publishers
538 Hood Road
Markham, Ontario, Canada L3R 3K9
www.pembrokepublishers.com

Distributed in the U.S. by Stenhouse Publishers
480 Congress Street
Portland, ME 04101
www.stenhouse.com

e acknowledge the financial support of the Government of Canada through the Canada Book Fund (CBF) for our publishing activities.

We acknowledge the assistance of the Government of Ontario through the Ontario Media Development Corporation's Ontario Book Initiative.

Library and Archives Canada Cataloguing in Publication

Baskwill, Jane

Attention-grabbing tools : for involving parents in their children's learning / Jane Baskwill.

Includes bibliographical references and index.
Also issued in electronic format.
ISBN 978-1-55138-283-8

1. Educational technology. 2. Communication in education. 3. Parent-teacher relationships. 4. Teaching — Aids and devices. I. Title.

LB1028.3.B38 2013   371.33   C2012-907592-2

eBook format ISBN 978-1-55138-850-2

Editor: Kat Mototsune
Cover Design: John Zehethofer
Typesetting: Jay Tee Graphics Ltd.

Printed and bound in Canada
9 8 7 6 5 4 3 2 1

MIX
Paper from
responsible sources
FSC® C004071

Contents

Introduction

A number of years ago, I wrote a book entitled *Parents and Teachers: Partners in Learning* (Scholastic, 1989). At that time, many changes were taking place in the school system. The teaching of reading and writing had moved from a sight-word–driven, three–reading-group approach to a focus on meaning-making that started from the whole and moved to the parts. As what was then known as Whole Language gathered momentum among teachers and school districts, parents felt they were being left out of the loop. As a classroom teacher I realized I needed to improve my communication with parents in order to bridge the gap that existed between what were then perceived to be the attributes of the school (teaching and learning) and what were considered the attributes of the home (nurturing the child). This notion, firmly embedded in the culture of school and home, fostered and maintained a separation between school and home, regardless of the educational philosophy of the day, resulting in an ever-widening communication gap.

Now, years later, it is widely accepted that when home and school work together, children's learning improves. However, although this fact is readily acknowledged, communication between school and home is still often one-sided and remains a struggle for many teachers. And, as teachers know only too well, when communication breaks down it is the teacher who ultimately bears the brunt of parental concern or complaints.

In this day and age, parents hold greater expectations for their child's teacher. They expect to know what is happening in their child's classroom. They expect the teacher to be knowledgeable and to be able to communicate that knowledge clearly. They also expect that the teacher will not be the only one who knows the best way to teach their child.

Today's parents are much busier than the parents I worked with in my early years of teaching. They belong to clubs, often both parents work, and they enroll their children in a multitude of outside activities. They seem to have less time to devote to school matters. This is the age of cell phones and social media, of sound bites and eyewitness news recordings; therefore, the very definition of communication is changing. Boundaries that once existed between home and school are shifting and blurring, with teachers often finding that parents want to friend them on Facebook, follow them on Twitter, or phone them at home or on their personal cell phones! It is often hard for teachers to know how to handle these situations without alienating parents. Just as difficult is deciding what might grab the attention of parents in a positive and long-lasting way.

Although there have been many changes in education, not much has changed with respect to school–home communication. It is still an area that teachers agonize over and want to improve upon. Many of the teachers I work with have told me that they wonder if *anybody* out there (meaning parents) is reading or listening to their communications. They wonder how they can best involve parents in their children's learning.

It is my hope that this book will help teachers not only to find new ways to attract parents' attention to the communication tools they are already using, but also to find creative ways to engage parents' attention, helping them find the time and energy to do so. The benefits can be huge and greatly rewarding. And, ultimately, the one who stands to benefit most is the student.

1

The Parent–Teacher Partnership

Although children today live in many different types of family groupings, in this book we use an expanded definition of the term "parents" to refer to birth parents, foster parents, single parents, parents who are both moms, parents who are both dads, and other caregivers.

Parental involvement in children's learning often means different things to different people. For many teachers and parents, it means communication from the teacher about marks and behavior, and it means parent support to the classroom in the form of parent volunteers. The most common pictures that come to mind are face-to-face parent and teacher conferences, parents helping children with homework, and parents helping the teacher by going along on field trips or listening to children read in a corner of the classroom.

However, in order for real parent–teacher partnerships to be meaningful and long-lasting, as well as to have an impact on children's learning, teachers and parents need to understand the range of roles that parents can play in the partnership. Everything from maintaining a bedtime routine to giving praise and sending the message that learning is important can have a positive effect on parental involvement and, in the long run, children's learning.

From the research and from my continuing work with parents and teachers over the years I know that, in order to reach the most parents, methods must be varied and parents need to be kept informed. Parents need to know not only how their children are doing, but also how to best help support their children's learning and the variety of roles they may play in doing so.

I also know that not all parents are confident about the role they think they could or should play in their children's learning. This is why it is so important for you, the classroom teacher, to help parents understand the many ways they can help and the variety of methods you can use to communicate. Working as partners means building connections and forming relationships. Relationships between teachers and parents need to be purposeful and ongoing. Effective communication is the key to forming constructive and lasting partnerships. Now, more than ever before, there is research to help guide and support the important work teachers have been doing and still need to do with parents.

What the Research Tells Us

From research about successful parent–teacher partnerships we know that, when teachers are committed to working closely with parents and see this partnership as being beneficial to their own teaching and to student learning, the time and effort needed to establish such relationships is not seen by teachers as a burden. For these teachers, home–school partnerships are not an optional extra but are rather integral and essential to their core work of teaching.

Henderson and Berla (1997) state, after more than 30 years of research on the importance of family involvement in students' learning, "when schools work together with families to support learning, children tend to succeed not just in school but also throughout life." They go on to say

> The most accurate predictor of students' achievement in school is not income or social status, but the extent to which the student's family is able to:
> - Create a home environment that encourages learning.
> - Express high (but not unrealistic) expectations for their children's achievement and future careers.
> - Become involved in their children's education in school and in the community.

Henderson and Mapp (2002) published a synthesis of research that supports and expands upon how parental involvement is linked to student achievement. From the studies they surveyed they found that:

- When families are engaged in supporting their children's learning at home, there are links to higher student achievement.
- When family involvement at home is ongoing, there seems to be a protective effect on children as they move through the education system. The more families support their children's learning, the more their children tend to do well in school.
- With support, families of all cultural backgrounds, education, and income levels can encourage their children, talk with them about school, help them plan for higher education, keep them focused on learning and homework.
- Parent involvement that is linked to student learning has a greater effect on achievement than that which is more general. Most effective forms of involvement are those that help families gain specific knowledge and skills in order to support children's learning.

The authors also concluded from the studies they surveyed that relationships matter. In fact, they comment that the studies suggest that "the quality of the relationship influences whether connections…will be formed or sustained."

Thus the research supports that at the heart of any school–parent relationship is you, the classroom teacher. When you embrace a philosophy of partnership and see the responsibility for a child's educational development as a collaborative enterprise, you have a powerful impact on the parent–teacher relationship, one that holds the child at the centre of all education decisions.

When you think about it, this notion is key. It is what you have in common with all parents, regardless of their background or current involvement. It is the common ground upon which you can build their trust and confidence in you as their child's teacher and in their ability to support their child in his or her learning journey. What you and the parents have in common is the child. When you keep the child as your focus, you can work together to find solutions and actions for even the most difficult challenges.

The Extended Family Framework

When building a more sustainable and rewarding relationship with parents, a helpful starting point is to create a picture in your mind of the type of relationship you are striving for with parents. Once you have this picture as your goal, it will be easier to make a plan for getting there.

Grade 4 teacher Alex, like many teachers I have met, was feeling frustrated by what he felt was a one-sided relationship with the parents of his students. It seemed to him that he was doing a lot of work for little benefit that he could see. It was at this point he realized that thinking about what the parent–teacher relationship might look like was a first step in moving forward more purposefully and effectively. He told me this:

> I never could understand why I wouldn't get much buy-in from parents when I spent so much effort on creating detailed newsletters, invited them to special back-to-school evenings, or even wanted them to attend parent–teacher conferences. I found myself getting frustrated and thinking that parents today are too busy or that some don't even care. I started to think that what I was doing was old-fashioned and not modern enough for today's parents. It was getting me down. It was then that you said I should try creating a picture in my mind of what I wanted my interactions with parents to be like. Well, at first I thought only of negative stuff and thought I couldn't get to the picture I want. You know, a more positive one. But then, when we talked about closely-knit extended families, I was all over it. That was just what I needed to help me get out of my negative thinking about parents. It helped me see the possibilities.

As Alex indicates, one way to view communication between parents and teachers is to see it as being similar to the communication that goes on among members of a closely-knit extended family. Within the concept of an extended family, reciprocal communication becomes a natural expectation. I first developed this concept when I was a classroom teacher. It became the guiding principle upon which my communication with parents is based (Baskwill, 1989). Over the years, as a teacher, principal, consultant, and university professor, I have maintained my belief in this framework. New ways of communicating, along with older ones, fit into this model.

Communication within an extended family is a concrete picture with which teachers and parents can identify, and it is an experience that many can draw on, directly or indirectly. Consider what you and a parent might expect of each other if you were a member of a family. You would expect each other to

- Keep in touch: face-to-face or by e-mail, snail mail, social media, phone, Skype
- Share news: day-to-day happenings, stories and anecdotes about the adults or children in the family
- Be open and honest: express feelings, share information, ask questions
- Trust: trust in the relationship to get you through the rough patches
- Respect: treat each other with mutual respect and courtesy

The picture of your relationship with parents and the value you place on communicating with them changes when it is viewed as a reciprocal relationship built on trust and empathy. In such a relationship, effective communication is a two-way street that results in understanding between partners. In this type of relationship, the blame game is seldom played, as the partners work together to find solutions to problems. The framework of the closely-knit extended family frees your thinking so you can explore a variety of ways to make communication easier, more frequent, and a regular part of the school experience. It can also help you feel more comfortable and confident with the initiatives you put into place, because you know that everything you choose is built on a solid foundation.

Communication Plans and First Impressions

Communicating with parents requires a variety of approaches. Just as the children in your classroom are individuals with their own unique learning needs and interests, so, too, are your students' parents. You will find that some parents will be avid readers of your newsletters or notes. Some are hands-on and will attend workshops and meetings. Others will be most attentive when communication is in the form of e-mails or Tweets. This doesn't mean you have to do all of these things. However, it does mean that one size does not fit all, so you will need to consider what you can do and how you might go about it.

Some forms of communication will be easily folded into what you already do; others will require a bit more effort and planning. However, just as with all subjects in the curriculum, if you want to make certain something will happen, you have to plan for it. So, too, with communicating with parents. It is helpful to map out a year of communicating, indicating what tools you plan to use, how often and for what purpose, along with what parent-focused events you plan to have.

The tools might include newsletters (paper or electronic), a website, pamphlets, etc. Events can include meet-and-greets, special class events, work parties, etc. Some tools, like newsletters, will happen more regularly (e.g., a monthly newsletter) than others (e.g., a meet-and-greet that might happen only once in September).

Laying it all out in advance, in an orderly fashion, allows you to stay organized and be prepared. You will be able to see at a glance if you are going for long periods of time with little or no communication or if you are relying solely on one communication tool. You will also notice if a month is getting too crowded or if your overall plan is unbalanced. In addition, having a plan alleviates some of the stress you might feel around communicating with parents and gives you confidence in your ability to do a good job. The good thing about using a planning template is that it can be a work in progress, growing and changing in response to the needs of both you and your parents.

See page 14 for a template for the Communication Planner.

The planning template on page 14 will get you started. Begin by filling in what you already do or what you think you want to do. Perhaps you know you want to have an event in December but don't know what that will look like. That's okay. Just record "*event — tba*" and come back to it once you have decided. You can add ideas from this book or ones that colleagues share.

Continue to map out your plan for the year. As you work on your curriculum planning, look for ways to link your parent communication to your students'

SAMPLE COMMUNICATION PLANNER

Month	Tool (e.g., newsletter, Facebook, e-mail, etc.)	Purpose	Event (e.g., Literacy Night, Math Take-home, etc.)	Purpose
August	*Letter*	*Intro me and my classroom*		
September	*Survey Newsletter*	*Get contact info*	*Meet-the-Teacher*	*Curriculum night — school-wide*
October	*Dialogue Journals*	*Start with parents who missed Meet-the-Teacher*	*Spooky Family Literacy Night*	*Literacy stations — questioning and comprehension*

learning. School-to-home connections are ways to enlist parents' support for literacy learning in purposeful, curriculum-related ways. They are opportunities to engage parents' help to reinforce a strategy or concept you have taught.

Try to link home connections to your mini-lessons:

1. When using a touchstone/mentor text as a model in your writing lessons, demonstrate the concept with the students and provide an opportunity for them to practice individually or in small groups: for example, using a nonfiction/information book, teach students the use of a KWHL chart to activate prior knowledge, set the purpose for reading, and stimulate further interest in a topic.

See *Books as Bridges* (Baskwill, 2010: 71–101) for a more detailed look at home connection activities and sample letters to parents.

2. Then send home an activity that mirrors or extends students' learning using the same concept or strategy: a letter that informs parents what a KWHL chart is, explains why you are teaching its use, and describes how they can use the chart or the questions the chart poses when reading a nonfiction book with their children at home.

Some teachers will feel comfortable jumping right in and scheduling a number of new ideas along with what they already do. Others will want to tread a little more slowly and put their toes in the water before they actually wade in. Do what's right for you. Chances are, once parents start to respond favorably to your efforts, this response will provide you with all the encouragement you need to keep going and to seek even more ways to effectively communicate with parents.

See page 15 for the Individual Event Planner.

It is also helpful to set up a Communication Binder in which to put a page of description, notes, reminders, or things to remember to do or not do for each communication tool or event; see the Individual Event Planner on page 15. If you keep the Communication Binder up to date, you can make use of it year after year and save yourself a lot of work in the long run. It is a convenient spot to keep reminders and feedback about how your efforts have been received and to remind yourself of the *dos* and *don'ts* for next time. Gathering this data in one location helps you to make an informed decision regarding any changes you may want to make to your communication planning along the way.

SAMPLE INDIVIDUAL EVENT PLANNER

Event: *Family Science Night*	
Date: *October 18*	**Time:** *6:00–7:00*
In Advance • *Prepare and send invitation* • *Collect materials for science stations* • *Prepare direction cards for science activities* • *Create Pinterest board for families with science activities*	
On the Day • *Set up stations* • *Send home reminders via Facebook and bookbag notices* • *Have feedback forms available*	
Feedback Comments • *Mostly positive* • *Several families requested additional activities they could do at home on the same topics*	
Next Time • *More links to science info for each station*	

See page 16 for the Communication Tool Summary Sheet.

Similarly, when you use a communication tool for the first time, it is a good idea to create a way to record the individual tool, the number of times it is used, and notes pertaining to its success, including pertinent feedback. The Communication Tool Summary Sheet (see page 16) gives you an overview of a specific tool and affords you an easy way to track its effectiveness. Each time you use a tool, enter the information on the Summary Sheet for that tool in your binder. As you look back over your Summary Sheets you will be able to readily see how often the tool was used and when. The comments you note will allow you to monitor feedback. Recurring issues or compliments, as well as comments you have received from parents, will help you make decisions on a tool's use in the future.

SAMPLE COMMUNICATION TOOL SUMMARY SHEET

Tool: *Facebook*

What it was used for	Date Used	Successful?
Announcement: Meet-the-Teacher	*Sept. 12*	*15 families went to it*
Photos of new learning stations	*Sept. 28*	*Yes!*
Concert reminder for Nov. 10	*Nov. 8*	*19 families came*
Volunteer request	*Dec. 2*	*2 volunteered*

Feedback Comments
- *15 families said they liked the photos and reading about the class activities on Facebook*
- *5 families said they didn't know how to use it so haven't signed up*
- *1 worried about personal information getting into wrong hands*

Next Time
- *Hold a Facebook info/how-to session before starting the Facebook Group*
- *See if anyone is interested now*

Making a Good First Impression

Start with Your Classroom

A great place to demonstrate to parents that you value their participation is your classroom. Create a Communication Station where you can post information of interest to parents just outside your classroom door. As this will be the first thing parents see when they approach your room, it should be attractive, eye-catching, and labeled so parents know it's for them.

If you have a bulletin board outside your classroom, consider using it as the focal area of your station. Use the station for posting class activities and information. Use prints of digital photos to add interest. Divide your station into sections:

- **Featured Curriculum Focus:** Feature one curriculum area by highlighting the theme or topic you are currently working on and some of the learning activities in which students have been/will be engaged.
- **Try This at Home:** a related activity families can try together; for example, the directions for a kitchen science activity or a book-related craft. This is a perfect way to link to the curriculum you are already doing.
- **Book Recommendations:** This is a little like a "book talk" on a poster.

Recommend a book you have just discovered or one related to the featured curriculum area. Parents appreciate knowing what books you recommend. This is also a perfect place to direct them to the public library to look for the book or others on the same topic or by the same author.

- **Newsletter:** a copy of your current newsletter. It never hurts to have a variety of places where parents can access your newsletter. Putting it online, sending a hard copy home (to those who can't access it online or to those who prefer to have it in hand), and then posting it on your Communication Station ensures it will be visible and will most likely be read.
- **Have You Seen These?:** Some notices never reach home or are read by one spouse but not the other, so post a master list of important notices you have sent home.
- **Can You Help?:** a good place to request volunteers or to seek materials for curriculum projects.
- **Calendar:** Post a monthly calendar with important dates and information highlighted. If you already have one on your website or as part of your newsletter, you can start with it and add or change it as needed. This serves as a reminder for any parents who come to your classroom before or after school.

A small table can be placed beneath the board if you have room. On it you can place a school map, sign-up sheets, requests for arts and crafts materials, pamphlets of information of interest to parents (e.g., packing nutritious lunches, safety information, etc.). Some of these materials can be obtained free of charge from public-health, mental-health, and other related agencies.

Make sure you include the Communication Station in your Communication Planner.

You will want to make sure that your Communication Station stays current and up-to-date. Decide how often you will change your information—once a week, once a month, or as needed. If you allow information to remain too long, parents will stop looking at it. Photos of your classroom in action related to the featured curriculum area will keep parents' interest and draw them back to the Station time and again; however, be sure to follow your school/district policy regarding photo permissions.

Photo Board

If a Communication Station is not something you feel you can tackle at the moment, or if you do not have an appropriate location for it, why not put up a photo board? Select pictures of your classroom in action. Captions are a nice touch and will help parents connect your photos to the learning going on in your classroom. Try to include a few photos that show you. Remember, these should show you in action, teaching in a variety of contexts.

The adage "A picture is worth a thousand words" holds true for your photo board. Pictures showing you and your students in many different teaching and learning activities will help to instil in the mind of your parents the image of your classroom in action. Make your photo board eye-catching by mounting your photos on an attractive background. Engage your students in the picture-taking by making the camera available for them to take photos of interesting classroom learning events as they occur.

Communication Planner

Month	Tool (e.g., newsletter, Facebook, e-mail, etc.)	Purpose	Event (e.g., Literacy Night, Math Take-home, etc.)	Purpose
August				
September				
October				
November				
December				
January				
February				
March				
April				
May				
June				

Pembroke Publishers ©2013 *Attention-Grabbing Tools* by Jane Baskwill ISBN 978-1-55138-283-8

Individual Event Planner

Event:	

Date:	Time:

In Advance

On the Day

Feedback Comments

Next Time

Pembroke Publishers ©2013 *Attention-Grabbing Tools* by Jane Baskwill ISBN 978-1-55138-283-8

Communication Tool Summary Sheet

Tool: _____

What it was used for	Date Used	Successful?

Feedback Comments

Next Time

Pembroke Publishers ©2013 *Attention-Grabbing Tools* by Jane Baskwill ISBN 978-1-55138-283-8

2

Getting Started

Introducing Yourself

Meeting parents for the first time is just like going for a job interview: to get your foot in the door, it is important to make a good first impression. Many primary teachers send a letter to a child starting school or to the parents, introducing themselves and welcoming the students and families. Nina, a Grade 5 teacher, learned the importance of a positive first contact using this approach.

> I used to be so nervous when I would meet parents at our "Meet-the-Creature" night. I had trouble sleeping and never felt the event was really comfortable for parents or for me. Then a colleague of mine suggested I do what the Primary teachers did and send a letter home to each of my students' parents introducing myself and welcoming their child to my classroom. It was amazing how many parents came up to me and said how much they appreciated that letter. They said they were lucky to have a teacher who cared enough to send them a letter.

A letter sent by snail-mail is an attention-grabber in this day of e-mail and social networks. If you use brightly colored envelopes and print your message on patterned printer paper, it will be sure to be noticed when it arrives. Keep in mind the following:

- The tone and content of your letter is important. It should be friendly and free from "teacher speak."
- Address it with the name of the student whenever possible (i.e., *To the Parents of*_____).
- The first paragraph should welcome families to your class and briefly introduce yourself (number of years of experience, a bit about your philosophy, etc.).
- In the second paragraph, assure them you are looking forward to a great school year. In the third, explain how you have prepared for this year: perhaps you read a book, attended a PD session, or made some enjoyable learning materials.
- If you know when you will have your first Meet-the-Teacher or Open House, include the date and time. Tell parents how much you are looking forward to meeting them. If there will be additional information sent out, let them know when and where they will find it.
- Refer to an enclosure you include with the letter: tips for getting your child ready for the first day, a list of children's books you recommend, educational websites, etc.
- Thank them and let them know you hope to see them at the Meet-the-Teacher event.

Make certain to check over your letter carefully. Ask a friend or family member to read it over. Check and recheck! The last thing you want is to have a typo or spelling error in your first communication. Keep your letter to no more than a single sheet of paper, both sides.

Dear Parents of _____

I am very pleased to have _____ in my class this year. I have been a Grade 5 teacher for six years and enjoy working with this age group very much. Over that time I have learned that children learn best when they are able to take an active part in their learning and when they can connect their learning to real-life events. I also feel it is very important to get to know each individual student and the ways he/she learns best.

I am very excited to start this school year. Over the summer I have been reading some exciting professional books about how to motivate children to read more. I hope to share what I have learned with you and my students. I know that when students are motivated to read and when they read books that are of interest to them, their ability to read improves. I plan to have my students read a lot!

Our school is planning its first Meet-the-Teacher night on September 14th from 6:00–8:00. Hopefully you will put this on your calendar so you can attend. I am planning a surprise for that evening that you will be able to take home and share with _____, so please check our class website to learn more.

I have attached a Kids Picks booklist that I put together with my last year's students. These are books that the students felt I should recommend to my next class as being great reads. I hope you will share this list with _____. I have other lists of great reads that I will be sharing over the course of the year. If your child has a title that that he/she would like to share, please send it to me and I will add it to our website under the Kid Picks section.

Once again, I look forward to working with you and _____ over the coming year and to meeting you at Meet-the-Teacher. Should you have any questions or wish to reach me in the meantime, e-mail me at teacher@staff.ednet or telephone the school (XXX-XXX-XXXX) and leave a message. I will get back to you as soon as I can.

All the best,

Meet-the-Teacher Nights

Meet-the-Teacher, sometimes called Back-to-School, nights are a chance for parents to meet their children's teacher and are a way for schools to assemble the parent community and to solicit help on committees and school projects. This kind of event is also usually designed to give parents information on the curriculum to be covered at a particular grade level. These evenings have become so commonplace that in some cases the number of parents attending has fallen off considerably; in others, parents attend but the event itself is less than satisfying for both teachers and parents. Although the structure of this evening might need to be somewhat uniform, as it is a school-wide event, it is still possible for you to put your own unique stamp on your Meet-the-Teacher event.

Send a Personal Invitation: Personalize an invitation to be sent above and beyond the one sent by the school. An effective invitation might use student drawings as decoration or have each student create the card for their own parents. If you can, arrange for some free giveaways for attendance (e.g., discount coupons from local restaurants, a book, back-to-school trinkets from discount stores).

You're Invited
Moms and Dads of Room 2M
To the Valley School
Meet-the-Teacher
When: Wednesday April 17
Where: Valley School Gym
Time: 6:00 followed by
a visit to Room 2M at 7:00
Please come and meet my teacher!

Some teachers don't want to be in the pictures that are shown to parents. But the purpose of the slide show is to make a good first impression. Part of achieving this is conveying that you are a professional with knowledge and skills that will help you do your job to the best of your ability and with the best interests of your students in mind. You send a different message if you are missing from the photos altogether.

Show What Goes On in Your Classroom: Prior to the evening, take photos of various activities that go on in your classroom to put on a computer for parents to view as a slide show while they mingle and wait for you to start. Take lots of photos and show the children in a variety of learning situations. Have your students, a colleague, or the principal take photos of you in action to incorporate. Think of the advertising you see on TV—images convey a lot of meaning, so be aware of this when selecting your photos. Put some family-friendly music with your slide show and—voila!—you will have made a lasting impression with the families of your students.

Provide Snacks: Have a few munchies on hand. There's nothing like a little snack to give comfort and set a friendly tone.

Take-Home Communication Plan

Don't try to do too much in your take-home communication plan. I have seen detailed coil-bound booklets and three-ring binders sent home. All this information often takes a lot of time to prepare and can be overwhelming for parents. Parents have told me they don't read these larger tomes and may not even keep them for reference. They are too impersonal.

For some schools, communication plans are sent home to parents at the start of each school year. This becomes a "contract" of sorts, in that it outlines for parents what is covered in the curriculum, if there are special events or activities that will happen during the course of the year (e.g., testing, a camping trip, etc.), and how communication can be initiated.

Prepare a short version of your communication plan to hand out at your first parent evening. It should include a brief welcome note, key information about

For a sample brochure, see page 21. Print each half on one side of a piece of paper; fold along broken lines to form brochure.

If you have families for whom English poses difficulties, try to find someone to translate your pamphlet so you can send it home in the languages of your students' families.

The sooner you get to know your students' parents, the more effective your communication will be. For instance, if you know that a number of families prefer to receive updates and information via social networking, it might influence you to create an account for this purpose, as you know that parents are likely to access it. No sense creating an account and *then* trying to convince parents to start using it!

each curriculum area, and a bit about your homework policy and the types of assessment you use. You should also include a few words about how you will communicate with parents and let them know how to contact you. Some teachers I know use the pamphlet feature on their word processor to create a concise, attractive brochure for parents. Print your hand-out on colorful paper and supply parents with a magnetic clip so they can hang it on the refrigerator at home for handy reference. Make mention of this feature in your talk—after all, you want parents to keep your contact information handy. What better place than on the fridge!

Some teachers distribute a bookmark that lists the variety of communication strategies they will use and URLs, as appropriate. The bookmark puts all communication possibilities in one piece that can be put on the refrigerator for reference as needed. It can be produced on a word processor and revised in response to feedback and need as communication tools change.

At your Meet-the-Teacher event, be sure to cover the points in your hand-out as you talk about your classroom and anything else you want parents to know. Be sure to emphasize that it is important for parents and teachers to work together to find communication strategies that work and that you will seek feedback from them to discover what combination of these is most effective.

Gathering Data

It is important to gather from your students' families data that will help you decide how to best communicate with them. Some teachers feel this is intrusive; however, I have found that parents are happy to share information when they understand why you are asking them for it. When the information is used to better communicate with them, respond to their needs, and help them support their children's learning, they readily provide you with it.

Ask parents to fill in a brief questionnaire; see the Parent Contact Information Survey on page 24. Your survey should include information that will help you with your planning; i.e., how parents wish to be contacted or kept informed, what educational/parenting topics might be of interest to them, any special information you should know about their child or their family situation. You might find it helpful to organize this information on a Parent Contact master form, as shown in the sample here.

SAMPLE PARENT CONTACT AT-A-GLANCE

Student	Parent/ Guardian	Home phone	Work phone	E-mail	Travel	Newsletter	How to Contact
Carlos Alvarez		*123-4567*	*234-5678*		*bus*	*e-mail*	*e-mail*
Brenda Bishop		*345-6789*		*mombishop @gmail.com*	*pick-up*	*child*	*cell phone*
Martha Davidson		*456-7890*			*walk*	*child*	*Skype*

Science
- Simple Machines
- Properties and Changes in Materials
- Weather
- Body Systems

Social Studies
- French and English Settlements
- Exploring Our World/Societies Over Time
- First Nations

Health
- Circulatory System
- Healthy Relationships
- Lifestyle Choices
- Personal Development

Art
- Line, Colour, Texture, Shape, Size

Keeping in Touch

Keeping in touch with you is a priority. I hope to use a variety of ways to stay in touch. Some may work better for you than others. I will count on your help to tell me what is working and what is not. I look forward to working with you.

I can be reached at the school (school phone), or by email at (teacher's email) on our Facebook site: **5B's Best** at www.facebook.com or send a note with your child. Also look for our "News in Brief" that comes home each month. The full newsletter can be read online at www.valleyschool.5B@ednet

Elm Street Elementary School
2011–2012

Class 5 Barlow

A sneak peek inside our classroom...

Dear Families,

Welcome to 5 Barlow! We have a very busy and exciting year in store for us!

I am thrilled to be teaching your child and will do my best to inspire and nurture a love of learning.

I look forward to working with you this year. Thank you for your support!

Homework

Students are required to read for 15 minutes each night. Your child will bring home a just-right book from their book box to practice. Have your child read aloud to you, a sibling, a pet, or even a stuffed animal!

Reading Logs are due on Fridays!

English Language Arts
Reading
Daily Read Alouds, Shared Reading, Reader's Theatre, Literature Circles
Speaking and Listening
Sharing Ideas, Group Discussions, Presentations, Speeches
Writing
Poetry, Mystery Stories, Persuasive Writing, Research, News Reports
Word Study
Word Wall, Word Patterns

Assessment

Many forms of assessment will be used to track your child's progress including:
- Observation
- Conferencing
- Individual and group work samples
- Interviews
- Experiments and projects

Mathematics

The elementary Math program includes four strands:
1. Number Concepts/Number Relationship Operations
2. Patterns and Relations
3. Shape and Space
4. Data Management and Probability

The Math Program is active! Students are engaged in daily hands-on experiences and will have opportunities to question, reflect, discuss, write, and use physical materials to enhance their learning. Communication of their ideas is emphasized.

SAMPLE PARENT VOLUNTEERS AT-A-GLANCE

Student	Volunteer?		Special Interest
	Yes	No	
Carlos Alvarez	✓		Mom is a nurse: will do classroom first-aid talk
Brenda Bishop		✓	
Martha Davidson		✓	
Ian Faquerson	✓		Dad: will help with woodworking large or small

SAMPLE PARENT WORKSHOPS AT-A-GLANCE

Student	Homework Tips	Family Science	Math Strategies	Reading Motivation	Other	After School	Evenings	Saturday
Carlos Alvarez	✓	✓		✓				✓
Brenda Bishop		✓	✓			✓	✓	
Martha Davidson	✓	✓	✓	✓			✓	

See page 24 for the Parent Contact Information Survey; pages 25–27 for forms for Parent Contact At-a-Glance, Parent Volunteers At-a-Glance, and Parent Workshops At-a-Glance.

Remember to explain to parents that you are gathering this information to be able to communicate with them more effectively and to get some idea about what might work best for them when you are scheduling. Let them know that you will do your best to offer a variety of ways to keep them involved and informed. Some teachers include the questionnaire in their introductory letter; others ask parents to fill it out at the Meet-the-Teacher event. Surveys and questionnaires like this allow you to easily see who is able to come to school to help and the optimum times to invite parents to come to school, and allow you to make more appropriate choices when deciding on what communication tools and events to use or plan.

You can keep track of the responses on a simple Communication Tracking Sheet (see page 28) for easy reference. Responses and the tracking sheet should be put into your Communication Binder.

See page 28 for the Communication Tracking Sheet.

Getting Feedback

After each of your events, gather more information that can help you as you plan in the future. It is important to try to figure out if there are obstacles keeping some parents from participating. Keep track of who attended, then follow up on those who did not. Following up with a phone call allows you to

- pass on important information to those unable to attend
- send the message that their participation is important

If you can't reach a family by phone, send a letter to catch them up on what they missed. Enclose the hand-out.

Once again, it is about going the extra mile. If you let parents see that communicating with them is important in your eyes, then communicating with you will become important in theirs. Be sure to record the information on your Individual

Event Planner sheet (see page 11 for more on the Individual Event Planner) and add it to your Communication Binder for future planning.

It helps to keep an open mind about why parents may not have come. There are many things that keep parents away; e.g., no child care, lack of transportation, misplaced note, work, etc. Try not to listen to negative talk about individual parents or families. Very few parents don't care. There are usually other reasons for their lack of participation. Some parents worry that they don't have anything suitable to wear or that they can't speak English well enough. Some may even think that they have all the information they need because they have another child in the school. By gathering useful information about parents' preferences and the barriers and challenges that might interfere with their involvement at a particular time, you will be able to modify and change your approach and increase parental support and involvement.

Parent Contact Information Survey

Dear Parents:

Please complete the following in order to make our communication between home and school easier.

Student's Name:

Parent/Guardian #1 Name:

Home phone/Cell phone:	Work phone:

E-mail:

Parent/Guardian #2 Name:

Home phone/Cell phone:	Work phone:

E-mail

How does your child usually get home?

☐ takes the Bus ☐ parent pick-up ☐ walks

In what way/s do you prefer to receive newsletters and notices from me:

☐ via your child ☐ by e-mail

How would you like me to contact you?

☐ e-mail ☐ cell phone ☐ home phone ☐ work phone ☐ Skype

Here's how you can reach me

School Phone: E-mail:

From time to time I will be offering workshops for parents. In what topics would you be interested?

☐ Homework Tips ☐ Family Science ☐ Math Strategies
☐ Motivating Your Child to Read ☐ Other (please suggest others)

Indicate when you prefer these workshops to be offered:

☐ After school ☐ Evenings ☐ Saturdays

I sometimes need volunteers for class trips or special projects, and to help making classroom materials. If you would like to find out more, please check one:

☐ Yes, please. ☐ Not right now.

Many parents have special interests, hobbies, or jobs they would be willing to share with the class. Please indicate what you would be willing to share (e.g., making bird feeders, work as a nurse, etc):

Interest/Hobby	About My Job

Thank you for taking time to fill this out. Please send it back to school with your child.

Sincerely,

Pembroke Publishers ©2013 *Attention-Grabbing Tools* by Jane Baskwill ISBN 978-1-55138-283-8

Parent Contact At-a-Glance

Student	Parent/Guardian	Home Phone/Cell	Work Phone	E-mail	Travel	Newsletter	How to Contact

Pembroke Publishers ©2013 *Attention-Grabbing Tools* by Jane Baskwill ISBN 978-1-55138-283-8

Parent Volunteers At-a-Glance

Student	Volunteer?		Special Interest
	Yes	No	

Pembroke Publishers ©2013 *Attention-Grabbing Tools* by Jane Baskwill ISBN 978-1-55138-283-8

Parent Workshops At-a-Glance

Student	Homework Tips	Family Science	Math Strategies	Reading Motivation	Other	After School	Evenings	Saturday

Pembroke Publishers ©2013 *Attention-Grabbing Tools* by Jane Baskwill ISBN 978-1-55138-283-8

Communication Tracking Sheet

| Student Name | Newsletter | | Contact | | | Workshop Preference | | | Volunteer | | Sharing | |
	Child	E-mail	E-mail	Phone	Skype	After School	Evening	Saturday	Yes	No	Interest	Job

Pembroke Publishers ©2013 *Attention-Grabbing Tools* by Jane Baskwill ISBN 978-1-55138-283-8

3

Newsletters

In preparation, gather information from parents and students as to what might go in the newsletter.

One tried and true way to communicate is to send out a classroom newsletter. The newsletter is a format with which most parents are familiar. Newsletters can be carried home by students, put online as part of the class webpage, or mailed to students' homes. This last option can be a bit costly but might be necessary for families without Internet access or when newsletters routinely do not make it home. In a newsletter you can give basic information about the classroom, let parents know what themes and topics their children will be working on, and provide tips and information.

Amelia, a Grade 2 teacher, dedicated a part of her newsletter to Tips and Information. She felt that covering this was important, as it allowed her to provide parents with information on a variety of themes and topics related to parenting and learning. After a while, however, she wondered if the topics she chose were ones that parents actually needed or wanted. She decide to solicit suggestions from parents:

> I wanted to make the Tips and Information section of my classroom newsletter more interesting for my parents, so I began sending home a request form at the bottom of the last page. I asked parents what topics or bits of information they would like me to include in the future. I was surprised by the number who filled it out and sent it back. I keep a running list of the topics, adding any new requests that came in. I am never at a loss for what to include, as I simply refer back to my list for ideas. Of course, if something comes up that is of immediate interest, I can include that, but having the list has saved me so much time. I don't have to try to come up with something I think parents will want. I have things I know they want.

Amelia discovered her students' parents were only too willing to make suggestions when asked. Taking up parents' suggestions in the newsletter attracts their attention and increases the likelihood the information will be read, especially if parents know these topics have been suggested by parents like themselves. Special sections, the visual appeal of the design, and photos and children's drawings all help to maintain interest that keep parents keen to check out the next issue of the newsletter.

Keeping Your Newsletter Fresh and Interesting

1. Decide how often you will send out your newsletter. It might depend on the existence of a school-wide newsletter and when that is issued. Some teachers

want their newsletter to match the school schedule, while others feel this can cause information overload for parents. In any case, committing to a specific number of issues will allow you to schedule it in your planning at times that work best for you.

2. Commit to the schedule and stick to it. Be sure to let parents know what the schedule will be, so that they know from the start of the year when they should look for the newsletter. A monthly newsletter is easy for parents to remember; another advantage is that you will have time between issues to gather news and information. Some teachers prefer a weekly or bi-weekly issue. These are usually both sides of one page, at most, and are most current. However, some teachers find putting out newsletters that often entails too much work. It is better to make a realistic commitment that you can keep, rather than have to make apologies for not keeping to the schedule.

3. Have regular sections in your newsletter. Include a calendar marked with days when students have no school, events that are for the whole school, events just for your class, and days when projects, assignments, take-home materials are due. Some teachers include a single-page calendar that can hang on the fridge at home for easy reference. Another regular feature might be children's books you recommend, websites that go with a particular area of study, and a section of tips and information. The tips can be as simple as ideas for nutritious lunches or as complex as a discussion on bullying. Plan out when you want to share the information. For instance, tips on helping with homework might be best given at the beginning of the year; summer reading or activity ideas will come toward the end of the school year. You might also have a section for student work, in which you share poetry, a brief news item, tips for creating Science Fair projects, etc. If you choose to share children's artwork or poetry over the course of the year, be sure to include work by each student.

4. Give your newsletter a standard look. A banner and two columns work well for the main page. There are many templates online from which to choose; however, you might prefer to make your own using a word-processing program, tailoring your template to your own needs. Either way, format is as important as content.

Tips for Designing Newsletters

- Make your newsletter eye-catching.
- Include a photograph or two of students at work on group projects or engaged in everyday classroom routines. This helps parents picture in their minds the classroom in action; it might also remind them of the slide show from the beginning of the year.
- Decorate your newsletter with student artwork. Divide the number of students by the number of newsletters and make sure each student is represented.
- If photos aren't possible, have students draw pictures that can be scanned and inserted into your document—either will draw parents' attention to the newsletter.
- Make all section headings slightly larger than the text so they stand out. Change the font size for the highlighted sections so they will be slightly larger than the font you use for the body and easy to spot at a glance. The body of the text should be no smaller than 12-point type, as smaller type is more difficult to read.

- Don't use too many different fonts, as they will make your newsletter difficult to read. The banner should be one font; pick one for all the headings. Try to work in a bit of color, either by using a color printer or by having the students color the headings or graphics, especially if these are done in a bubble font. But remember not to overdo color, just as you limit choice of fonts.

5. Even if you have your students' names in your newsletter, you will want to have your name or the name of your class included (e.g., *SuperSix: News from Ms Soteck's Grade 6*). This helps it stand out as being from you and still allows you to include your students in the process.

6. Date your newsletter to avoid any confusion over how current the information is.

SAMPLE FIRST PAGE OF A NEWSLETTER

Mr B's Gr. 5 News

Welcome Back!

Welcome! I am [teacher's name] and I am excited about joining the [school name] community.

There are high expectations for the students in Grade 5. As the oldest in the school they will have lots of new and exciting things to learn about, as well as great opportunities to lead in and around the school.

If there are ever any questions please don't hesitate to call the school, write a note, or e-mail me at [teacher's e-mail address].

Website Update

The [school] website has undergone a redesign. Please check it out at [school URL]. Be sure to check out the class pages and keep checking back to see what is new and exciting at [school]. If you do not have computer access, please contact me to make other arrangements.

Agenda and Communication Bag

Your child has a new communication bag. Inside you will find a communication notebook and any notices from our school and classroom.

This will be one of the many ways we will have to communicate with each other. Please initial in the space provided daily and remind your child to have their bag each day

Special Reminders

- Pictures – Friday, Sept. 16th
- Check out our online calendar for more special dates in September!

Monday	Tuesday	Wednesday	Thursday	Friday
5 No School	6 First Day!	7 Return Forms	8	9

The main thing to keep in mind is to be brief. Better to communicate often with a one- or two-page newsletter than a lengthier one once a month.

The Newsletter as a Part of Your Classroom

The creation of your newsletter can become a teaching opportunity that is a regular part of your classroom curriculum.

Have a space on your whiteboard to record ideas or information you might like to include in your newsletter. If you have in interactive whiteboard, keep a file called *Newsletter*. Make a table with labels for each section of your newsletter. As something comes up that you think you might like to include in a newsletter, note it in your table. For instance, if you find a website associated with a science topic and you want to pass it on to parents, copy and paste the URL into your table.

Newsletter as Writing Opportunity

Depending on the age of your students, you can organize small groups to create the content for many of the sections, treating the publication like a class newspaper. The whole class can work on it or you can create groups at the beginning of the year, making each group responsible for helping with a particular issue.

Regardless of the age of your students, they can all have a hand in assembling the newsletter. You can add it to your list of classroom helpers or take a few minutes during the day to have each student pick up and staple their newsletter together.

THE TEACHER'S MESSAGE

It is important for you to be actively involved. Be sure to include a brief message from the teacher, usually placed just under the banner in the left-hand column. In the classroom, use it as an opportunity to share your writing process in a mini-lesson. Solicit suggestions and comments from the students. Over the course of the year, fold the writing of your newsletter message into mini-lessons on voice, ideas, organization, word choice, etc.

Some teachers give each student in the class his or her own one-page newsletter skeleton to complete. Basic information, like the message from the teacher, is pre-inserted and a section is left for the student to personalize. These teachers have incorporated the newsletter into their language arts program and link to mini-demonstrations based on the teacher's message feature.

Newsletter as Mini-Lesson

The day your newsletter goes home, use it as a mini-lesson so that all students have some idea of its contents and purpose. Students who have had a part in creating that issue can be responsible for sharing their section with the rest of the class. Allow students to ask questions about the content: *Why did you choose this topic? What information did you have to leave out because of space? Is there anything that surprised you while you were writing this? What suggestions do you have for the next person?* Take the opportunity to share the message you included and why you chose it. When students have been actively involved in the creation of the newsletter and understand why you value it, they are more likely to encourage their parents to read it.

Making the Newsletter Interactive

Newsletters too often become a ritual that teachers go through but parents seldom read. Try to find unique ways to make your newsletter more exciting. Remember, if your children are enthusiastic about it and its content, then likely their parents will be more committed to reading.

You can make this communication tool more interactive by including a simple tear-off-and-return form that helps parents do an activity led by their children— a scavenger hunt or puzzle based on the newsletter content, a survey (*Next month do you want our featured curriculum area to be social studies or health?*), or a request for information or suggestions (*Do you have any ideas for a concert theme? Can you recommend someone in the area who can talk to us about cooking safety?*)

Ask Me About… News Flyer

Teachers of young children, in particular, often hear the complaint from parents that their child comes home and has little to share about what he or she has done at school all day. In fact, many parents report that when they ask their child "What did you do in school today?" their child responds with "Nothing" or "Played." Diana, a primary teacher, came to realize how important sharing information about a child's school day is to a parent when her own child started school:

> I learned first-hand what parents of the children in my class were experiencing when I changed jobs to a different school from the one my son, Paul, attends. Now I was in a position to not know what went on in his day. To my surprise and frustration, he would give me detailed descriptions of each gym period and what he played outdoors at recess. However, when I asked what he did in math, the answer was usually "pages." And when I asked what he had read that day, he drew a blank. My questions put him on the spot and, even though I know better, I wondered if he was learning anything in school. His responses caused me to doubt the capability of his teacher.

This story shows the power a child's response can have on a parent's perception of the teacher. What can counter this long-standing issue between parents and children is ensuring that parents have enough information to be able to ask the right questions. When parents ask the right questions, children respond knowingly and enthusiastically. It becomes a much more satisfying exchange all around.

When thinking about how to support Diana and the many parents and teachers experiencing a similar communication gap with their children, I thought about the phone conversations I would have with my children when they were younger and I was away from home. At such times, my husband Steve would set me up with such prompts as, "Ask Nicholas about what happened to his bike." "Ask Amanda about what the coach said." "Ask Amanda-Lynn about the new child in her class." When I asked a question based on a little prior knowledge, the result was a flood of conversation on the part of the child. I was then able to comment easily, listen supportively, and ask questions of my own. Even conversations between adults are far more interesting and productive when there is some common ground on which the conversation can be based.

Monthly newsletters, although informative, do not solve the "What did you do today?" issue. They provide a recap of old news or are an update of coming events, but do not meet this particular need. What is needed is a way to give parents insider's knowledge, at least for a while, until they and their children can establish a more satisfying school communication routine.

A single sheet provides more than enough space without overloading parent or child.

I worked with Diana and some of the other teachers in her school to try out what I called an Ask Me About... news flyer. As we experimented with what this might look like, we found the solution to be very simple and effective. The teachers began to send home a weekly flyer, hand printed on 8½" x 14" paper.

We decided to hand print them because they had a more personal quality that way. We also decided to decorate each issue with children's drawings. When the page was ready, teachers asked individual children to draw particular illustrations for the sections. For instance, for a section about writing instruction, a student might be asked to draw a picture of the children at their table working on their writing. The children drew with pencil on pieces of paper just big enough so that, when trimmed, they would fit in a corner of the section. We found that young children were quite eager to do drawings for the flyer. The finished pictures were glued onto the master and photocopied on bright paper for each child to take home.

See page 36 for a template you might use for an Ask Me About... news flyer.

The teacher briefly goes over each issue of the Ask Me About... flyer with the class. This doesn't take much time and allows children to go home expecting to talk with their parents about what they have been doing. The flyer highlights class activities over the course of the week and gives parents just enough information to enable them to ask a question that will get more than a "nothing" response.

We built in specific prompts. For example:

- *Ask me about our Writing Time. We do it every day and it is when we write about our own ideas.*
- *Ask me about the science activity in the Discovery Centre. It involves water!*
- *Ask me about the jungle that is growing in our room!*

We tried to keep the focus on the learning that was going on. All the teachers agreed that, when parents get upset or feel they are out of touch, they worry about academic progress and whether the school is teaching the right things. Their frustrations grow and are magnified when they speak with other parents

Diana and another teacher used a preparation period at the end of the week to write the text, while the other two teachers relied on doing the text at home over the weekend.

who feel the same. Finally their frustrations can end up in confrontation. The Ask Me About… news flyer served as a proactive way to allay any parents' fears that might exist.

Feedback from the parents was very positive and inspired the teachers to continue. Whether you send home a news flyer weekly or bi-weekly will depend on the feedback you get and your ability to work it into your week. You will need to schedule a time when you can sit down and create the flyer.

The news flyer works to keep the information current, while producing a manageable communication tool that speaks directly to parents and children. Many parents reported they were saving the newsletters in their child's memory box as the flyers were effective in capturing their child's school year. They also recognized that teachers were making a special effort to keep them informed and to help them better communicate with their children about what they do at school.

SAMPLE ASK ME ABOUT… NEWS FLYER

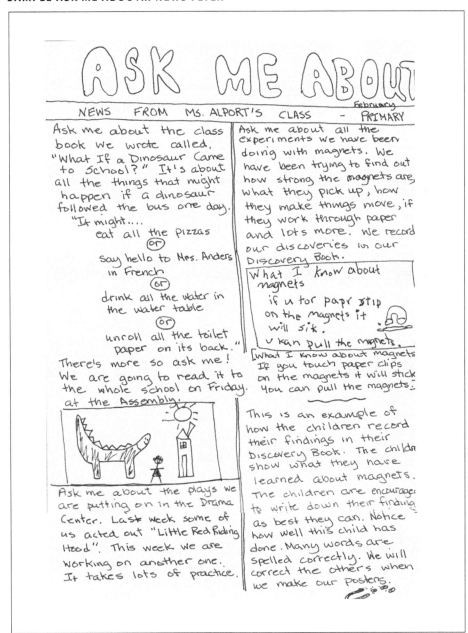

Ask Me About… News Flyer Template

Ask Me About	
News from (Teacher's Name)'s Class	**Date:**
Message to Parents	

Ask Me About (language arts topic)	**Ask Me About** (a station or centre)
Ask Me About (math concept)	

Ask Me About (a class activity; e.g., D.E.A.R.)

Ask Me About (books we have read: list books read aloud)

Ask Me About (student news)	**Ask Me About** (writing: new strategy, class book, etc.)

4

Day-to-Day

There are a variety of formats for communicating information between teacher and parent. Most encourage two-way communication by including some form of response from the parent, from a signature to a written response or exchange of information. Some, like the agenda, are used with the entire class, while others, such as the pass-along book or dialogue journal, can be used with selected students for a specific purpose.

Each of the communication strategies in this chapter asks parents to be actively involved in discussing and learning about their children's learning development and creates a bridge between home and school, providing a way for information to be shared. Since they occur over a period of time, there is an opportunity for thoughtful, in-depth sharing to occur.

Agendas

Student agendas, planners, or homework notebooks are usually used by teachers to help keep parents informed about their child's homework and long-term project assignments. They act as an organizational tool as well as representing a skill students will need as they progress through school. You can have your students purchase an agenda or you can create one just for your students. The important thing is to inform parents of the importance of the agendas and the purpose for which you are using them.

Be sure that you and your students use agendas or homework notebooks daily.

Lisa, a Grade 5 teacher, realized that she could make this tool more effective by creating her own homework notebook:

> I used to have my students' parents buy an agenda on their own for their children to record homework in. I found this to be a problem, as each book was different: some had more room to write, some showed the whole month at a glance. There was no consistency. So I decided to save my parents a lot of money and standardize our homework notebooks by making my own. Now I can even do mini-lessons using the organizer. Also, my students' parents are a lot happier to not have to pay out money for a book that we end up not using most of the pages in.

You can make your own agenda:

• Use the template on page 49: each page covers a two-week period
• Enlarge and copy on both sides of 8½" x 11" paper: this will give you four weeks on one sheet of paper.

You can have your students personalize the covers of their agendas with their own drawings or special stickers.

- Copy the appropriate number of pages for the time period you have decided on.
- Create a cover out of card stock.
- Place cover outside pages; fold pages and cover in half along broken line; staple on the fold.

Some teachers create a new agenda each term. That way, if it goes missing, it is not costly to replace.

The Homework Communication Centre

See page 49 for the Weekly Homework Notebook Page Template.

Lisa used a one-inch binder for her homework notebook, which became a homework communication centre, with plastic page protectors into which important notices, letters for signing, or marked assignments could be placed. From time to time, included in the homework notebook to be taken home would be tip sheets for parents and students about studying, nutrition, safety, books she thought her students would enjoy reading, extra-curricular programs, etc.

Here is how to make a take-home homework communication centre for you and your students' families:

- Ask each family to provide a one-inch (2.5 cm) three-ring binder. Suggest that they get the kind that can have a cover page inserted.
- Provide an eye-catching cover page. You can create an individualized page for each child with his or her name on it, or have your students create their own cover pages.
- Divide each binder into sections. You can purchase dividers or cut letter-size file folders on the fold and punch three holes in each sheet. Label each section:
  Section 1: *Current Week's Calendar*
  Section 2: *Parent's Signature Sleeve*
  Section 3: *Homework Papers*
- Write a letter to the parents explaining when they should expect their child to have homework and that this is a special notebook for the homework assignments.
  Current Week's Calendar. Ask parents to keep this in the binder for the week and to check it regularly for assignment due dates. Let them know that each student should bring the binder to school each day.
  Parent's Signature Sleeve. Let parents know that anything requiring their signature will be placed in this sleeve.
  Homework Papers. This sleeve contains homework papers or notices that need to be completed. Let parents know these items should be returned in this sleeve.

Most parents will recognize the work you have done and will appreciate the organization and the routine. However, if you undertake to create such a tool, it is important that you follow up each day with your students. Nothing is more frustrating for parents than to keep up their end of the bargain, only to find that the papers they signed or put back in the binder were never seen by the teacher.

The Friday Folder

In this variation of the homework notebook, the communication is sent home in a duotang folder that has pockets in the front and back. As the name implies,

A designated basket or bin in the classroom provides a place for the Friday Folder to be kept until needed.

it goes home every Friday. Some schools have made the Friday Folder part of their school improvement plan, with folders going home in each classroom every Friday. The standardization establishes a weekly routine for parent–teacher communication.

As with the communication centre, inside the Friday Folder are samples of student work for the week, information needing to go home from the school or directly pertaining to the classroom, and brief anecdotal comments the teacher wishes to share (e.g., Good News or Positive Praise forms).

Parents are encouraged to read over the materials and remove the contents. A recording sheet is placed in the front inside cover; parents are asked to sign and date the sheet each week. The Friday Folders are returned to the teacher on Monday. It is important to follow up with parents who have not returned the folder, have not signed their child's folder, or who have returned it without removing the materials sent home for them to keep.

Pass-Along Books

The pass-along book is a ruled notebook that travels back and forth between school and home. In the book, teachers and assistants share information about the child's daily activities and behavior, and parents also use the book to comment.

Pass-along books are a way for parents of a child with behavioral or learning needs to keep in touch with their child's teacher, usually on a daily basis. It provides much-needed and current information about how the child's day has gone. This is particularly important for maintaining consistency when implementing behavioral or learning goals. The book can be an agreed-upon strategy at an educational team meeting.

Implementing this communication tool might not be necessary for some parents, but for those who are concerned or anxious, or who have children with whom they have difficulty communicating (such as a child on the autism spectrum), this book can provide an important link to the classroom between home and classroom. If the child has a bad night or if there is something happening in the child's life later in the day, it is helpful for you to know about it so you can interpret appropriately any behavior you notice; likewise, you can share classroom events the parents could use a heads-up about.

Donelda is the parent of Nicholas, a Grade 4 boy with a global learning delay. The pass-along book helps her share insight into her child's language processing and receive feedback from his teacher. The extract here is part of a longer entry in the pass-along book in which Donelda shares a conversation she had with Nicholas about some of the children in his class. A new girl had joined the class and Nicholas said he liked her. Donelda tries to help Nicholas describe his classmate, Stephanie:

…We started talking about Stephanie, what color her hair was, if it was short or long, if she was tall or short. Then I asked him if she was chubby or skinny. Nicholas started laughing and he laughed until the tears rolled down his cheeks. When he had calmed down I asked him what he was laughing about. He said "chubby" was just such a funny word.

Mariana, Nicholas' teacher, responds:

I couldn't help but laugh out loud as I read your story. Nicholas has been enjoying the sound of words here in the classroom too. Words like "fuzzy," "itchy," and "scrumptious" have set him laughing, as he enjoys the sound of the word and tries to say it for himself. I must admit, it is a thrill to see him playing with language and enjoying it so much. He has come a long way! He has been reading joke books to us and wants to share his favorites with anyone who will listen. Nicholas is showing us that he understands the language of jokes and knows how they are supposed to work. This also tells me that his comprehension is there as well.

The pass-along book has allowed both parent and teacher to collaborate on the learning events they have each witnessed. The teacher shares her observations and what they tell her about the child's development as a reader and a learner. Both parent and teacher come away with a more complete picture and a better-developed theory about Nicholas' progress.

There are a few things to keep in mind about initiating the pass-along book:

- Clearly establish what information will be communicated, by whom, and how often. You will want to communicate often enough for parents to engage in the process, but not so often that it becomes a burden. Every other day or twice a week is usually manageable, unless something comes up on an unscheduled day that needs to be shared.
- Keep the extended-family model in mind as you write. This will help you maintain the right tone.
- Look for the positive. No parent wants to read page after page of negative entries. Instead, try to balance bad news with something positive whenever possible.
- Use plain language. Avoid using "education speak."
- Schedule a time to write in the pass-along book near the end of the day. Some teachers have a silent reading period for students while they do the writing. Some assistants write bits and pieces throughout the day.
- Let parents know that, because you will be writing on the fly, your handwriting may not be as neat as when you have more time and that they might find the occasional spelling error. Stating this up front will garner parents' understanding right from the start. If you are a proficient typist or your handwriting is poor, you might want to use the computer for composing your news so you can print it out and glue it into the pass-along book.
- Arrange for completed books to be stored in the child's classroom file so you can see if an issue or event resurfaces and remind yourself of what was said previously.

Remember, it is important to always consider when a face-to-face meeting or a phone call might be more appropriate than a written exchange. If you notice the same question keeps reappearing or the tone of the writing seems to be confrontational or unfriendly, these are signs that a more direct means of communication should be employed. Try not to let things go on too long before you schedule a meeting or pick up the phone.

The Keep-In-Touch Book

A variation of the pass-along book that can be efficiently used with the entire class is the Keep-In-Touch (KIT) book. Inspired by a communication idea for adult family members to use to keep current with each other, the KIT book is a scribbler or notebook in which you can put a weekly letter to parents to update them on classroom events and activities. The letter should contain the learning focus for one or more curriculum areas and a brief paragraph about what is happening in the week coming up. Parents can also write notes or questions, and you can respond either in writing or with a quick phone call.

SAMPLE KEEP-IN-TOUCH BOOK LETTER: GRADE 5 INTERDISCIPLINARY UNIT

Hi, Everyone:

I am very excited about the new unit we will be starting in Science. We will be focusing on trees and how they are an important part of our ecosystem. We will learn about how to identify different kinds of trees by examining the ones we have here on our school grounds. We will take bark rubbings, gather a sample of leaves, and work on a field guide to the trees we identify.

As part of this unit, we will learn about photosynthesis and the role trees have in cleaning our air. We will also consider the many ways in which trees are important in our lives. In addition, as part of Language Arts, we will write poems and descriptions of our trees and create posters to inform the rest of the school about the importance of trees.

In Art, we will go outdoors and sketch our trees. Inside we will use these sketches to create a large mural of a forest containing all the trees we have been studying. We will create short plays as a way to show others what we have learned. Look for an invitation at the end of this unit to come and view our work.

You can help by encouraging your child to read about the topic. If there is an item in the newspaper or a magazine related to trees, please discuss it with your child and encourage them to bring it to class. If your child reads anything online or from the library about the topic, please encourage them to share it with us. Finally, if your work or interests are related to this unit (e.g., gardener/nursery worker, forestry worker, artist, musician/singer), please contact me so we can discuss how you might share your knowledge or talent with us.

I hope you will enjoy this unit as much as I hope your children will. I look forward to sharing more with you in the near future.

Since this letter is describing an upcoming major unit of study, it is longer and has more detail than some KIT book entries that might follow. Unlike a newsletter, the KIT book allows you to focus directly on the curriculum and the current focus of study in particular curriculum areas. It is organic, dynamic, and very much in-the-moment.

Dialogue Journals

Dialogue journals are a tool that many teachers use in the classroom to foster teacher–student and/or student–student communication. As their name implies, they are usually lined notebooks in which ongoing written conversations are held between teacher and student. They are, by their nature, a place for students to share with their teacher their thinking on a variety of topics. During a designated writing period (usually once a week) students write in their journals about news they have, something they wonder about, or their thoughts on a book they are reading. The teacher reads each student's entry and then responds to the student, writing in a conversational tone.

Now some teachers are also using dialogue journals outside the classroom to foster parent–teacher communication. The format is similar to that of the dialogue journal used with students:

- The teacher selects a notebook that will travel back and forth with the child when teacher or parent makes an entry.
- The writing is conversational in tone.

These dialogue journals provide a means for teachers and parents to carry on a conversation over time about issues related to children's academic and social growth. When done well, the interaction is natural, individual, and, in some cases, thought-provoking. Conversations of this nature let parents know their input is valued; they go a long way in establishing a trusting relationship between parent and teacher.

Margaret, a Grade 3 teacher, overcame her apprehension about dialogue journals by devising a manageable system for using them. She explained it to me like this:

> When I first thought about using dialogue journals, I didn't feel confident. I had tried them before in my Grade 3 class, but I didn't keep them up and quickly my students lost interest. I couldn't imagine what I would say to parents. I went through all the normal *what-ifs*: *What if I can't keep up? What if parents ask me something I can't or don't want to answer? What if the parents think I'm prying into their private business?* In the end, you convinced me to give it a try and I'm glad I did. Because I gave them out to families over the course of a month, my fear of not keeping up was put to rest. They came back, one on this day, one on another, and so on. As long as I responded to the journal the same day it came to me, I could manage easily. In fact, I set aside a few minutes after the children left for the day to answer any journal that had come in that day. That way I wasn't tempted to put it off or let it get put aside because I was tired. I also didn't have to worry about what to say—I simply commented on parents' observations or responded to their questions. Sometimes I added an anecdote about something their child said or was working on. My responses have improved with practice. As for privacy, I think parents have learned to trust me. I never share their journals unless they want me to.

Margaret discovered that her organizational strategy helped to keep things manageable when not all families sent the journals back on the same day. She also learned that her worries about how to respond were groundless, as she simply responded to what the parents were initiating—just as she would if the parents were on the phone or dropped by the classroom.

For parents who are reluctant or too shy to ask a question face-to-face, the dialogue journal provides a perfect tool for their voice to be heard. In addition, some parents for whom English is not their birth language welcome the opportunity to practice their English writing skills. Some teachers, whose schools have access to translators, invite parents to write in their first language if that is more comfortable for them. The journals are then translated, as is the teacher's response.

It is important to stress the conversational nature of the writing. Help parents to think about dialogue-journal writing as talk written down. Try to respond to each entry clearly and concisely as possible, striving to maintain the tone of a friendly letter.

Most of the time, your journal replies will support parents' observations. The observations they make about their child's literacy development are often insightful. Through your response, try to confirm what the parent has observed and share with them what meaning you make from it.

SAMPLE ENTRIES IN A DIALOGUE JOURNAL

January 19: Angie (Artie's Mom)

Artie doesn't do much writing at home. Does he at school? At home he likes to draw pictures which tell stories though.

January 20: Mrs. Morton (Artie's Teacher)

At school, when Artie writes, he also uses his drawings to tell his stories. I have been encouraging him to try using his letter sounds to write down something about his picture. Right now he will label his drawings (*TRTL* = turtle, *FOCS* = fox) without help and without me asking him to. This is a good sign. He is starting to feel more confident writing on his own and he is beginning to realize that the story can also be in his words. If we encourage him gently and are patient, I am certain we will see his writing grow as he puts it all together.

January 25: Angie

Today, when we were reading "Where the Wild Things Are" Artie said, "The pictures always go with the words."

Artie's most extensive writing I have seen so far:

Artie Svns is 5 A HOF (Artie Stevens is 5 and a half.)

Picture drawn of a *PAPE* (puppy) with speech balloon with *"Waof!!!"* in it.

Exciting! – NHS (Artie's dad)

January 26: Mrs. Morton

Most of the writing I see Artie doing now is similar to what you have noticed—a drawing and a labeling of that drawing. However, just as in the January 25th entry, I also see him now able to put together strings of words to make sentences about his drawing. He seems to be really into writing now. He wants to write more and is interested in how to spell more and more words. He uses the short labelings to experiment with letters and sounds and, as he recognizes those short labelings are successful (he can read them, I can read them, you can read them), he is becoming more and more confident and so he tries longer groups of words and sentences. It is pretty exciting watching him put it all together! His writing shows that he is able to use consonants and vowels. He knows words have these and is getting closer and closer to standard spelling as he changes around the vowels he uses and compares his version to words he recognizes in the books we read to him or the "just right" books he reads himself.

P.S. January 25th was an exciting entry. Artie's awareness about the pictures and words always going together really shows he is working out the "system" of how this type of book works. Thank you for collecting and sharing this important moment!

Sometimes your response will be a few paragraphs, at other times more extensive, depending on the question. It might be more important to address the message between the lines and to respond with concrete examples. The following is an example of an entry Mrs. Samivor, a Grade 4 teacher, received from a family concerned about what their child was reading. Although the note was asking for suggestions, their underlying concern was over whether or not their child was going to continue to progress if he read only comics. It was the implied concern that the teacher chose to respond to.

SAMPLE ENTRIES IN DIALOGUE JOURNAL

Parent Entry

Del has been very excited about the comic books he has been reading in school. He seems to always have his nose in a book now, but we are concerned that they may not be challenging him enough. We haven't seen him read a real book lately, just the comics. I know it is important for him to read what he likes—and he certainly likes these—but we want to get him interested in more than just this. What can we do about this?

Teacher Entry

It is understandable that you would think the graphic novels and comics are not challenging Del as a reader. However, let me reassure you that the books Del is choosing are anything but simple.

As you know, Del was a student who didn't like to read anything that looked like it had a lot of text or chapters. Even though he could read almost at grade level, he sought books that were well below. He often chose early chapter books rather than anything more challenging. He also didn't pay attention to the meaning of what he was reading. He often read any word whether it made sense or not.

Since beginning the unit on graphic novels and comic texts, Del has been hooked. He is reading graphic novels with more complex story lines and gaining confidence as a reader. And now he is writing them! Ask him to tell you about his Comic Life project.

You will remember that, at our last conference, I mentioned how hard it was for me to get him to write more than a few sentences. Now he is coming to me with ideas for graphic novels he wants to write. He has made several shorter comics and now wants to tackle something bigger. This is so exciting. I am hoping that, as he has more success with these types of books, eventually I can move him to a bridge book—one that has some comic-like illustrations along with more novel-like chapters. I don't want to push it just yet.

I am sending home the first book of a trilogy that Del is working his way through for you to have a look at. If you would like to talk about these types of books or to see some of Del's writing and read more of the books he has read, please contact me and we can set up an appointment. I hope this answers your concern.

In this example, the teacher has left the door open to a face-to-face meeting if the parents feel it is necessary. It is important with messages like this one to decide if the message warrants a follow-up meeting or phone call. However, keep in mind that if you follow-up too often parents might stop writing, as they start to feel that every time they write something you will require more from them in some way.

Over the years, as I have helped teachers get started with dialogue journals, I have seen the benefits to both parents and teachers. On paper, something happens. Writing helps both you and your students' parents examine an issue from more than one point of view. Writing allows parents time to think things through as they collect their thoughts and try to express themselves clearly. Through dialogue journals, parents draw on the strength of observation, a skill they have naturally cultivated in terms of their children over the years. With your help, they can extend and expand their skills and apply them to their understanding of their child's learning development.

Tips for getting started with dialogue journals:

- Choose an inexpensive notebook with lines and a modest number of pages. Choose something that is inexpensive but easily recognizable. A scribbler is a good choice because it is associated with school, doesn't have too many pages, and, if it goes missing, can be easily replaced.
- Label the cover of the journal with something like the following:

  Ms. Fell's
  Dialogue Journal
  With the Parents of
  Karli Adams

- Create a letter explaining the purpose of the dialogue journal (see sample letter below). Glue the letter to the inside front cover. Even though you will likely be explaining the purpose of the journal in person, the letter serves as an easy reference for parents should they want to refresh their memory about its purpose.

SAMPLE DIALOGUE JOURNAL LETTER

Dear Parents:

At school I see the ways in which your child is growing as a reader, a writer, and a learner. Every day I learn something about your child's interests, as well as observing how he/she learns best.

At home, I know that you are seeing many things, too. You hear your child reading, you help your child with his/her school work, you take your child places or look for new activities that will interest him/her.

I think it would be a great idea if we shared some of that information with each other. That is why I have given you this journal. It is a place for you to jot down any things you notice or hear your child say that you would like to share. Perhaps your child is really excited about a new interest or hobby. Perhaps you have a new pet or your child has watched a TV show about something that has fascinated him/her. If I know about this new interest, I can find books that he/she might like.

By pooling our information we can foster and encourage your child's love of learning and we can make sure your child's learning is on track.

In this day of e-mails, it may seem odd to suggest we keep a journal together, but I find that writing by hand gives me time to think about what I want to say. It is also portable. You might be able to find some time to write while you are waiting for one of your child's activities to end or waiting to be called for an appointment. The number of times you write is up to you. Write once a week, once a month, once a term, or as much as you like. I will write back whenever I hear from you. Since your child will be bringing the journal back and forth between home and school, please be sure to let him/her know when it is in the book bag. I'll do the same.

I hope you will give this dialogue journal a try and work it into your family's schedule. Please be assured that what you write will be kept confidential and will not be shared without your permission. Thank you for considering this request.

I look forward to hearing from you.

Sincerely,

Try to give the journals to parents in person at the first Meet-the-Teacher or whenever parents come to school. They are more likely to participate when you make personal contact. They will also be able to ask questions if need be.

Be patient. Give parents time to write to you. Some might be hesitant because they think they can't write well enough or don't know what to share. Keep inviting these parents to participate when you see them and put reminders in your newsletter. With the author's permission, share a few entries from another parent's dialogue journal or create a sample with a common question parents have asked in the past and your response. Those who don't know what to expect can feel more comfortable once they have seen a sample. Keep the sample short and friendly in tone so it will not be intimidating.

An additional benefit to using dialogue journals is that, through them, you will come to know your students' families better than you have ever known them before. As well, parents will know you as more than just a name on the door or a face across the table. They will see you as a person who shares an interest in the development of their children and who is committed to their education.

The Student–Teacher–Parent Journal

Involving the students allows you to incorporate the principles of student learning journals along with parent-communication goals. Students share their reflections on learning and get feedback and support from both teacher and parent.

A variation of the dialogue journal is the student–teacher–parent journal. On a predetermined day, students write for 10 minutes on a topic related to their learning; e.g., if they are meeting a learning goal they have set for themselves, what their current reading interests are, current curriculum units that are underway, etc. They then take their writing home to their parents. Some teachers who employ this tool send the journal home on Fridays. Over the weekend, or whenever the journal goes home, the parents add to the journal, responding to their children's writing and/or writing something new. The teacher responds to each of the journal entries by the following Friday. Making this a weekly event allows you ample time to respond. Often a discussion thread begins one week and is carried on over the course of several.

In this sample entry, Raylene, a Grade 5 student, is responding to a prompt from her teacher, Mr. Watson, asking about students' favorite character in the book they are reading.

Student Entry

I really liked the character Coraline from the book. At first I didn't think I would like her or the book at all. I wanted her to have some kind of magic powers but she didn't. I thought she wasn't going to be able to save her parents or herself from the other mother. I was disappointed at first because I like characters who are magical and she wasn't. But then I found myself liking her because she was brave and wasn't afraid to keep trying. In the end she turned out to be one of my favorite characters. I was kind of sad when the book ended because I liked her so much. What did you think of the character Coraline, Mr. Watson? Did you like her all the way through? I think you should read this book, Mom. I bet you will like it. Then we can talk more about this character. I wonder what you will think of Coraline's mother and her other mother. It won't take you long to read it I bet. Maybe you can borrow a copy from Mr. Watson.

Parent Response

Coraline must have been an interesting character to have made you change your mind about her. I know how much you like stories with magic in them. Did this one have any magic at all? You said Coraline didn't use magic, but did anyone else? I am curious about the "other mother" bit. I definitely want to read the book so we can talk about it more. What do you say, Mr. Watson? May I borrow the book?

Teacher Response

Mrs. Marster, you can certainly borrow the book. I will send it home with Raylene. I loved this book. In fact, I waited to watch the movie until I had read the book. Then, after watching it, I was amazed at how they were able to take the writer's words and bring them to life. I know what you mean about Coraline. I kept waiting for her to show some magic power or to get some powers—maybe from the cat. I was actually glad in the end that she didn't. The author was able to keep the reader wondering how she would outsmart the other mother. She certainly managed to outthink everyone! I liked her all the way through but started liking her a lot once she started to realize her other family wasn't a perfect as they first seemed. Can't wait to read what you think about her, Mrs. Marster, after you have read the book.

When you first start out using student–parent–teacher dialogue journals, it is often helpful to begin with language arts. Children's reading and writing progress is usually of paramount importance to parents, and it makes a good starting point for students as well. Ask students to write in response to a prompt:

- *What was the most interesting thing you learned during our mini-lesson today during language arts?*
- *What strategy did you practice during your independent reading? How did it work for you?*
- *Tell us about the main character in the book you are reading.*
- *What strategies do you use when selecting a new book to read?*
- *Tell us about what you like to read and why.*

Eventually you might want to expand the prompts across curriculum areas. For example:

- Ask students to make observations or raise questions from science experiments you have done in class. Students can also talk about the process they use when making predictions or recording their observations.
- Have students write an explanation of how to solve a specific math problem in order to demonstrate to their parents how it is done.
- In social studies, ask students to share an interesting event or describe a historical figure you are studying.

Student–parent–teacher dialogue journals can be easily incorporated into your classroom in the following ways:

- Mini-lessons can focus on topics for reflection, the structure of a reflection, and how to respond to comments.
- Students can be given opportunities to share their entries with their peers and seek feedback.
- Use what you have learned about the student's learning growth, preferences, and challenges when planning for instruction.

A variation on this journal format is for you to write the first entry about what you have noticed about a student's learning or a question you have about it for the student; e.g., *What kinds of supports in the classroom help you learn best?* The student responds to your comment or question and then the journal is sent home for parents to contribute to the conversation from their perspective.

Day-to-Day Communication Tools

Remember, it is important to tailor the communication tools to your students' families. One size does not fit all, so don't expect that any one form of communication will be taken up by everyone. Extend the invitation and enjoy the dialogue you have with those who participate. Consider modifying the tool; e.g., you might offer parents the option of an e-mail version of the dialogue journal.

Weekly Homework Notebook Page Template

Monday	Tuesday	Wednesday	Thursday	Friday
Monday	Tuesday	Wednesday	Thursday	Friday

Pembroke Publishers ©2013 *Attention-Grabbing Tools* by Jane Baskwill ISBN 978-1-55138-283-8

5

Learning Nights

Parents play an important role in supporting student learning. Strong connections between home and school are needed to ensure that parents and teachers are working together to advance the learning development of children. You can strengthen these connections by offering curriculum nights and Saturday sessions for parents/guardians and/or by supplying take-home activities that connect with classroom learning outcomes and objectives.

Family Nights

Traditionally, family nights are school-wide events to which families are invited. Often parents and children come to the school to watch a movie, play games, sample curriculum activities, or participate in athletics or playground games. These are usually opportunities to build a positive school climate while providing time at school for parents and children to participate together in a fun event. Although some of these may be curriculum-related (e.g., Family Literacy Nights), most are social gatherings.

If you really want to communicate to parents that their partnership is important for the academic success of their child, consider organizing family nights for the parents of the children in your class. These nights should focus on how parents can support student learning in specific curriculum areas.

There is nothing wrong with building a positive school climate through school-sponsored family events. However, family nights, when offered by the classroom teacher, have an important role to play in the parent–teacher partnership and can enhance communication and send a powerful message to parents that learning is valued. Some teachers, like Cathy, a Grade 3 teacher, lack confidence to undertake such an initiative. Cathy found a way to take an important first step:

> For the longest time I shied away from doing any evening or Saturday workshops for my students' families. I didn't feel confident standing up in front of a group of parents. I didn't feel that way around children, but I convinced myself that being in front of adults was something I wouldn't be good at, so I didn't do it any more than I had to. But then my principal and I were going over my personal learning goals and I thought: *Why not put family nights as this year's goal?* I am so glad I did. I started with topics I was most comfortable with, like my Read Around the Room night. With the help of my students I set up stations to show the reading we do in all the curriculum areas. The idea was for parents to circulate with their children from station to station, read a book, and have a brief conversation about the book with their child based on the prompts I had on the activity card. I started the evening by talking about the importance of comprehension and how, by sharing stories with children, parents can help them better understand the text. The feedback from the families has been awesome. I am so glad I took that first step.

By making family nights part of her personal learning goals for the year, Cathy was not only able to take that important first step, but she was also able to enlist the support of her principal and access resources available to her for that form of school-based professional development.

When you create your communication plan (see Chapter 2), be sure to schedule at least one family curriculum night each term. Some of the teachers I work with have found that they receive such positive feedback following one of these nights that they are keen to try another. Be careful to consider what else is going on at the school when scheduling your nights, as you don't want to conflict with a school-wide event.

Hosting a Family Curriculum Night for Parents

When you offer family curriculum nights for parents you are communicating a lot more than information. You are demonstrating that you value their partnership and are willing to share what you know with them. These fun-filled evenings provide a structure for families to comfortably explore, experiment, and talk about the curriculum area being focused on. This will carry over to their understanding of information you send out in newsletters and other communication tools.

Families that participate in these evenings have a greater understanding of the importance of the subject in their child's life. Parents and teachers can then work together to create an enthusiasm for learning in all subjects and to encourage students to build a strong foundation that will serve them well in future learning experiences. Family curriculum nights also help parents keep in touch with the curriculum and feel part of the day-to-day teaching and learning going on in your classroom.

Effective family curriculum nights create an environment in which families can participate in a hands-on learning experience. Families also have the opportunity to experience how you plan and organize the curriculum, featuring linkages across curriculum areas.

Planning Successful Family Nights

Successful family nights

- **engage families.** Families enjoy the excitement of participating in a learning community. Organize family nights around a topic or theme and invite active participation that is nonthreatening.
- **invite exploration and learning.** Family nights provide an organized learning event in which families have the opportunity to explore their understanding of a curriculum concept. Learning stations are perfect for this. Although they require a bit of advance preparation, learning stations that are well organized, with clear instructions and ample materials, minimize frustration and enhance the learning experience for everyone.
- **connect with your classroom instruction.** Family nights provide you with an opportunity to showcase what you are teaching in the classroom. This will enable parents to better interact with their child at home and to use the experience to create opportunities for further investigations at home.

- **are easy to organize and facilitate.** Family nights should not become elaborate productions. They should be easy to plan, host, and facilitate. Materials and activity instructions should be prepared in advance, in plain language, to ensure a successful evening. Provide refreshments whenever possible.
- **encourage positive attitudes about the curriculum area being featured.** Keep activities interesting and authentic. Choose ones that allow for interaction at a variety of skill levels. Help families make connections to everyday life by sharing websites, magazines, or TV programs on the theme or topic.
- **are inclusive.** Be mindful of the needs of all of your families. Translate materials whenever possible or invite someone from the community who speaks the language to assist with translation if need be.
- **seek feedback.** At the end of the night, distribute a simple feedback form to help you plan for your next event. See page 62 for the Family Night Feedback form.

Family curriculum nights around a particular topic or theme can be either one-off or part of a series. For some curriculum areas, you might offer several sessions featuring a particular aspect of the curriculum each night. Sometimes you might want to invite parents to come without their children, especially if the information you share does not lend itself to a fun family event; e.g., topics about behavior, special needs, drugs, etc.

At other times it might suit your needs to have the parents with you for the first half-hour while their children are in another room doing a related activity. This requires another pair of hands. Sometimes a colleague or parent volunteers might help out. Also remember that curriculum sessions can be run on a Saturday during the day if that suits you and your parents.

Choosing the right topics for a family night can help you successfully motivate parents to attend your events. You can solicit suggestions from families in a survey or on a tear off portion of your newsletter (see page 33). Here are a few tried and true topics to get you started.

Project Night

Invite families to a session where they learn appropriate strategies for helping their children with a project you have assigned. Send the invitation home with your project assignment.

On the night, have samples of projects that have been done by students previously, along with your marking scheme or rubric, so parents can see the range of work and how it has been marked (be sure to remove students' names). Allow time for parents and children to plan their project, make lists of materials they will need, and develop a timeline for completion.

You might have materials available that families can use to start on their projects. If you have access to computers, they can be made available for those who need to do research. Parents will appreciate the opportunity to ask questions about what kind of help would be most appropriate. Often simply going over the rubric will help parents know what will need to be included. Working in a group setting allows children and parents to exchange ideas with other families. This session is particularly relevant if your school has a science fair or cultural exhibition in which children are asked to submit projects for evaluation.

Remember to take lots of pictures of parents and children in action at your family nights. With the families' permission, pictures can be posted on a bulletin board in the hall, on your website, or in your newsletter so other families can see what they missed and will be eager to participate the next time. They remind families who attended of the workshop experience.

Homework Help

Invite families to a session that focuses on their children's homework and how they can help them with it appropriately. Provide parents with strategies and techniques to help motivate and support their children with their homework assignments.

This session provides an excellent opportunity to engage parents and children in an activity in which they design a homework centre for their home. Have them begin by evaluating where homework is done and some of the pros and cons about their present homework location and habits. Parents and children can then decide where the best place in their home is to have a homework centre, what furniture they have that they can use, etc.

Discussing the homework centre is an opportunity to talk to parents and children about the importance of having a homework routine. Encourage them to use the centre as the location in which all homework is done. Suggest that as soon as children get home from school they should deposit their backpacks and school books there, making it easier to keep track of all materials and assignments. Parents will appreciate the opportunity to send children a unified message about homework and homework routines.

HOMEWORK HELP IDEA: MAKING A HOMEWORK TOOLKIT

Help families learn how to make a Homework Toolkit to help parents organize the supplies students need to make homework go more smoothly. Rather than having to hunt for pencils, markers, staples or other supplies, keeping a plastic container with an assortment of materials the child might need will save time and help avoid frustration on the part of both parent and child.

1. At the session, have parents and children make a list of the things they think would be useful to have in their Homework Toolkit.

2. If you are able to obtain a modest amount of funding, have parents put together a basic Homework Toolkit to which they can add supplies later.

Make-and-Take

Hold Make-and-Take nights during which families make a variety of home learning activity kits. Make-and-Takes are an extremely effective way to empower parents with the knowledge they need to reinforce the mathematics, science, and literacy strategies you use in the classroom. At the Make-and-Take, explicitly teach and model the focus strategy. Then guide parents to set up an activity they can use with their children in order to reinforce and practice the strategy with them at home.

Parents enjoy making activity kits, blank books, and games that can be used at home to support learning. Each Make-and-Take activity should have some connection to your curriculum outcomes or lesson objectives and should strengthen or extend those skills and strategies.

Make-and-Takes can be offered for your classroom alone or as part of a grade-level activity. How you set it up will depend on the number of participants you anticipate. If it is done as a grade level, you might choose to have parents rotate from room to room, with each teacher on your team presenting a different take-home activity to reinforce the theme, curriculum area, or skill.

You can help parents learn how to use storyboards and comics as a writing activity. At the Make-and-Take they can put together a kit with the materials they will need to do the activity at home with their child.

1. In advance, collect a variety of comic strips from the newspaper.

2. Prepare storyboard templates with the same number of spaces as in the comic strips you have collected.

3. Do a mini-lesson for parents. Briefly talk about the value of this activity in encouraging children's creativity and imagination through storytelling and writing, as a way to reinforce comprehension skills and retelling. Project a set of panels and lead the group in retelling the comic strip you have chosen.

4. Have parents assemble the take-home. Ask them to select comics from the ones you have provided that they think their family would like to use for this activity at home. They should also select the appropriate blank storyboard to go with the number of panels in the strip.

5. Have them decorate a manila envelope and label it *Comic Strip Storyboards*.

For more activities parents can do at home using comic strips and a sample storyboard template, see *Books as Bridges* (Baskwill, 2010) pages 50–51.

Family Science

When planning Family Science Nights, tailor them for parents and children of all ages. Feature hands-on activities that use simple, inexpensive household materials to explore the way that science plays a role in daily life. Stress that, to get involved in these activities with their children, parents do not need a background in science, only a willingness to become engaged and explore alongside their children. Make sure parents understand they can expect to have fun as they participate in science activities and learn science with their children. Be sure to plan for a minimum of an hour and a half for this event.

In advance, prepare the materials for one science activity that all families will participate in, or prepare materials for different activity stations among which they will rotate. Go over the activity and the directions with the group before having them try on their own.

Some topics that make for easy-to-assemble activities for a Family Science Night:

A nice keepsake to present to families is a small booklet of the science activities they have done, along with additional ones to try at home.

- **Let's Be Scientists: Using Our Senses** incorporates a variety of activities that ask parents and children to use their senses to complete a specific task: e.g., identify items by smell or taste alone. A great picture book for this is *My Five Senses* by Aliki.
- **Fingerprint Detectives** gives parents and children experience collecting and analyzing evidence as they collect their own fingerprints and compare them. Ed Emberley's *Fingerprint Drawing Book* is a fun way to end an evening of fingerprinting.
- **Float and Sink** engages families in activities in which they determine whether various objects sink or float in water. *Who Sank the Boat* by Pamela Allen is a great book to read to get things started.
- **Fun with Magnets** encourages families to think about how magnets are used, how they work, and why they are useful. A book to share as a launcher is *Mickey's Magnet* by Frankyn Mansfield Branley.

- **Kitchen Science** draws on the many science activities that can be done with everyday ingredients found in most kitchens; e.g., baking soda and vinegar volcanoes, invisible ink, rock candy crystals, etc.
- **Halloween Science** is a great way to link a holiday theme with a family science activity night: e.g., Halloween Slime from borax and white glue, a static dancing ghost using a simple balloon. Any Halloween story will help set the mood: a favorite of mine is *The Tailypo: A Ghost Story* retold by Joanna Galdone.
- **Stargazing** takes families outside under the night sky to involve them in the science of astronomy. A star chart, binoculars or a telescope, and perhaps a local expert make for a great family event. Activities can range from identifying constellations to the physics of the Universe. Assemble a number of nonfiction books for easy reference. Consider accessing Google Sky Map or a similar program or app for families to try out.

You can focus one night on a particular topic, with four or five stations with different experiments for parents and children to do together. Send home easy-to-read instructions so families can do the experiments again at home, along with others they can also try on the same topic.

Using Online Resources

There are websites you can use and direct parents to: e.g., the Parent Place at http://www.tryscience.org/parents/se_1.html and the Kitchen Pantry Scientist Blog at http://kitchenpantryscientist.com/

You can connect these websites to your classroom by showing students the activities that can be found there and suggesting they show the site to their parents. Send home a bookmark of your favorite science websites, a general one or one that has sites related to the particular topic of the evening. You can also put these links on your webpage. In addition, create a Pinterest board (see page 102) devoted to family science activities and information.

Family Math

Family Math Nights provide opportunities for parents and caretakers to learn about mathematical concepts their children are learning in the classroom, activities that can be used at home, and strategies to help children with their homework. Math workshops can also provide opportunities for parents to develop their own mathematical thinking and increase their knowledge of general math skills, while enhancing their understanding of how mathematics is taught in the classroom. Many parents feel inadequate when trying to help their children with math; math anxiety can prevent them from responding to children's learning struggles in appropriate ways.

Try to determine the challenges that parents face when they help their children with their mathematical learning. You might send home a survey or enlist the help of a small group of parents in determining what needs should be met during your Math Night.

Regardless of the topic or format for the evening, it is a good idea to begin with a brief introduction that includes a reassurance that parents do not have to be good at math themselves to help their children. A learning-station format is most appropriate for easing parents' anxiety. Set up stations with a math activity at each station. The idea is to make the stations fun and interactive. You want families to see math as enjoyable and something they can do in their daily life. Be sure to start the night with a basic introduction to the activities.

Family Math Nights can easily be linked to classroom work. The stations you create can be set up so that students can demonstrate for their parents what they are learning and can lead parents in a hands-on activity.

- **Wrap Around**: A simple but fun activity for families to try. This station requires index cards and scissors. The object of the activity is to cut the index card so it can wrap around a family member's entire body. Have parents and children work together to figure out how to accomplish the task.
- **Shopping Spree**: Give each family a price limit and have them prepare a shopping list from weekly grocery flyers. Instruct them to try to stay on budget, and provide a calculator for each family to use.
- **Speed**: A game in which two family members roll dice and everyone tries to quickly add up the numbers.
- **Card Games**: Each station teaches families to play a particular card game. You can use well-known games, such as Concentration or Go Fish, or ones that might be new to families. An example of a new game is the **Playing Card Adding Game:**

    1. Use cards in each suit from ace to 10.
    2. The first player draws cards and lays them face-up for all players to see. For younger children two cards are drawn; older children can draw three numbers.
    3. Everyone adds the numbers; the first to say the sum aloud gets a point.
    4. The cards are shuffled and play is repeated.

- **Manipulative Magic**: Set up each station with a different manipulative—pattern blocks, tangrams, unifix cubes, etc.—and prepare several sets of directions for using them.
- **Math Search**: Ask each family to look through newspapers and magazines to find numbers for a variety of things: a time, a date, the child's age, the parent's age, a number greater than or less than a given number, a temperature, a price, a graph, etc.
- **Geometry Hunt**: Go over a hand-out of basic geometric shapes with families. Wherever possible, use photos of real-world three-dimensional shapes to illustrate the shapes on the hand-out. In addition, try to have acutal objects on hand as examples; e.g., ball, ice cream cone, Toblerone box, sugar cube, toothpaste box. Families walk around the classroom and/or school and find examples of the geometric figures on the hand-out. A take-home activity would invite families to do a geometric walk around their house. Give them extra copies of the hand-out so they can fill them in at home.

FAMILY MATH IDEA: RESTAURANT MATH NIGHT

Learning activities with connections to everyday experiences are a way to demonstrate to parents how to reinforce and extend their children's learning during normal family events and outings. A restaurant activity is a perfect way to do this.

In advance:

- Make up menus and fill paper plates with images of main dishes and desserts—cut from magazines—to match the menu.
- Collect materials needed: play cash registers, note pads, pencils.
- Set up your classroom or other suitable space in your school with tables and chairs.
- Make up bags of play money: nickels, dimes, and quarters for K–Grade 2; add higher denominations for Grades 3–5.
- Arrange for students from your class (or another) to play hostess and seat families at the "restaurant."
- Arrange for other students to be wait staff and cashiers.

On the Family Math Night:

1. Families order from the menu.

2. The paper plates matching their order are delivered to each table.

3. The bill is made up.

4. The family adds the total bill and takes it to the cashier to pay.

FAMILY MATH IDEA: PICTURE BOOK FOCUS

This Family Math Night is centred on *Grandfather Tang's Story* by Ann Tompert, a story told using tangrams.

1. After reading the story to the families, provide them with sets of tangrams for exploration and storytelling. If possible, have multiple copies of the story for reference.

2. Parents and children retell the story, creating each animal using the tangrams.

3. Provide families with an opportunity to make their own tangram set from fun foam. Send home a package of tangram activities with each family.

Books to Use for Family Math Nights

Grades 4–6: Area and Perimeter

Burns, Marilyn. *Spaghetti and Meatballs for All!*
Mrs. Comfort arranges eight square tables for a family reunion, each with four chairs, so that all 32 guests will have a place to sit. But as guests arrive, they create havoc with their own seating plans.

Activity: Families can use square tiles or draw on squared paper to experiment with what happens to the seating when square tables are pushed together.

Kindergarten–Grade 2: Geometry

Emberley, Ed. *The Wing on a Flea.*
This book has brightly colored illustrations and simple rhymes. Children learn how common geometric shapes—triangles, rectangles, and circles—are found in the world around them.

Activity: Parents and children list all the things a shape can be; e.g., a triangle can be a hat. Families can illustrate their ideas using foam or paper shapes and drawings.

Florian, Douglas. *A Pig Is Big.*
The book opens by asking, "What's big?" and presents an exploration of things that are increasingly bigger and bigger—from a pig to a cow, car, truck, street, neighborhood, city, Earth, and finally the universe.

Activity: Families use measuring tapes to measure family members and compare various measurements; e.g., Dad's arm is longer than my arm.

Kindergarten–Grade 1: Time

Hutchins, Hazel. *A Second Is a Hiccup.*
This book explains units of time in ways that all children can recognize. It begins with *How long is a second?* and goes on to address the length of a minute, an hour, a day, a week, a month, and a year.

Activity: Create a list of timing activities for families to try.

Grades 2–4: Money

Axelrod, Amy. *Pigs Will Be Pigs.*
There's nothing to eat in the refrigerator, so the famished pig family decides to go out for dinner. But they don't have enough money, which results in a search throughout the house for coins and bills. Finally, they pig out at their favorite restaurant, the Enchanted Enchilada.

Activity: You can create an assortment of activities using money; e.g., families go on a scavenger hunt for hidden coins, then add up the money to see how much they have found.

Family Literacy

Families are often to unaware of how much they already do to support their children's literacy learning. Family Literacy Nights are a great way to celebrate those activities, as well as share new ideas.

There are many activities you can use to make Literacy Nights an enjoyable family experience that carries over learning from school to home. Make sure materials are easy-to-find and inexpensive, so that parents can easily replicate activities at home. In your opening, it is crucial that you help parents understand the importance of what they are about to do and how it relates to their children's literacy development. You can prepare a hand-out to underscore this.

Just as with other curriculum nights, you can organize your Literacy Night around a theme, strategy, or book. Organizing activities around a theme/topic allows you to choose a subject that is likely to appeal to parents and children, that will be fairly easy to organize, and that will be an instant hit. Some examples:

- **Cooking**: Invite families to bring a favorite recipe. Compile recipes into a book following the event. Provide an assortment of no-cook recipes, ideally ones that combine pictures with directions so that they will be easy-to-follow for adults who might not be proficient readers.
- **Skipping Rope Rhymes**: This activity pairs literacy with physical activity and fitness. Make sure parents understand the importance of rhyme and repetition, then have them learn the words along with the skipping or hand actions. You

If you prepare extra sets of directions for all activities, families can collect them and take them home for easy reference.

can use the gym or schedule this for when you can go outdoors. Teach your students the rhymes in advance and prepare a take-home for ready reference.

- **Games Night**: Board games are making a comeback. Collect a variety from colleagues, friends, or yard sales. Be sure to talk about the many skills children can learn by playing board games: turn-taking, strategy and problem-solving, reading, counting, etc.
- **Making Family Books**: Invite families to bring three to five photos of a family outing, vacation, or celebration. Prepare a storyboard on which families can plan their stories. Have parents transfer their story to a blank book you have prepared—8½" x 11" paper folded in half. When the books are completed, staple them and present them as a take-home.

FAMILY LITERACY NIGHT THEME/TOPIC IDEA: STORYTELLING

For tips and storytelling activities for parents see *Getting Dads on Board* (Baskwill, 2009) pages 33–35.

Storytelling is a perfect fit for families. Begin the night by telling a story to the whole group. If you are a bit nervous about telling a story you make up, you can project the pictures of a favorite story and retell it in your own words. Or you can invite a librarian or community storyteller to kick off the evening. Another way to start is to show a video (found online) of a children's storyteller or author: Robert Munsch (*Mortimer*) and Sheree Fitch (*There Were Monkeys in My Kitchen*) are always crowd pleasers.

After the opening, divide families among the stations you have created or lead them in one activity. Some possibilities:

- **Retelling Stories with Puppets**: Make a set of puppets for a favorite book and retell the story. Puppets can be made from pieces of card stock and glued to a craft stick.
- **Imaginative Stories with Puppets**: Make up a story by creating a set of puppet characters. Each family member makes his or her own puppet, then they all make up a story with all their characters in it. Puppets can be simple sock puppets or made from paper plates, bags, gloves, etc.
- **Conversation Starters**: Make a large picture of two story characters; they can be characters from the same story or from two different stories. Laminate the picture and hang it on a wall or easel where the rest of the materials—paper speech balloons, markers—are located. Invite families to make up a conversation between the two characters. Have them write on the paper speech balloons what each could be saying. Conversations are taped to the laminated board as they are created. Families can take home a smaller version of this activity with a picture of the two characters printed on card stock and smaller blank speech balloons.
- **What's Happening?**: Cut out interesting pictures from magazines or newspapers. Have families make up the story to go with each picture.
- **What's Happening in Our Classroom?**: Have a variety of photographs you have taken of your classroom in action. Children and parents tell each other what is happening in the pictures.
- **It's In the Bag**: Assemble paper bags containing 4–6 common items; it is good to have extra bags prepared so families who finish with one bag can go on to another. Have each family start a story: e.g., *Once upon a time there was a young boy/girl named _____. One day, as he was walking to school he came upon a_____.* Someone reaches into the bag without looking and pulls out one object the family must work into their story. The tale continues until all the objects have been worked into the story.

You can choose a topic or strategy you have been focusing on in the classroom—comprehension strategies, picture walks, retelling strategies, writing activities, genre study, etc.—and build activities around a favorite picture book. Choose a picture book that is a hit with your students. Regardless of grade level, picture books allow you do read the entire book and develop home connections for families to try on the Family Literacy Night and then do on their own at home.

> Wordless picture books provide a way to involve parents of all literacy levels in the reading of the book and activities that springboard from the reading. One such book is *Tuesday* by David Weisner. *Tuesday* is about how some seemingly ordinary frogs from a pond go on a magical adventure throughout the city. The story comes full circle with everything getting back to normal—almost. *Tuesday* is funny and highly entertaining for adults and children alike.

1. Project the story so all families can see it as you lead them in a reading of the story through the pictures.

2. Select a page from the book. Have families role-play a news reporter interviewing characters about what is happening. Provide simple props, such as a microphone, notebook, reporter's badge.

3. Have families retell the story from a different point of view. Provide a variety of tools for recording: paper and pencil, computer, storyboard, audio recorder, etc.

4. Assemble an assortment of wordless picture books for families to share together. Make a list of the books and post it on the wall. Ask families to vote for their favorite by placing a sticky note next to their choice.

If possible, have multiple copies of the story on hand, so each table grouping of families can have a copy to which they can refer.

5. Provide materials so families can create a 10 cm square (4" x 4") play-clay tile of their favorite scene from the book. Prepare cardboard squares on which to create the scene. Family members can collaborate to create one scene or, if you have enough clay, have each family member make their own. Empty CD cases are great ways to protect the creations; just be sure to cut the cardboard base so it will fit inside the case.

TIPS FOR FAMILY LITERACY NIGHTS

Special activities don't take a lot of time but can make your Family Literacy Night even more memorable:

- Borrow an idea from Family Literacy Day 2012 (ABC Canada) and create a passport for families to get stamped after completing each activity you have set up.
- Enter family names in a draw for a book at the end of the evening.
- Arrange a book swap: families bring a book and get to take a book home.
- Provide parents and children an opportunity to create a reading journal.
- Arrange a reading by a local author or invited guest – perhaps in costume!—to wind up the night.

For all of your family nights, make sure there are lots of take-homes and lists of URLs, books, and resources parents can consult for more ideas.

If you are interested in attracting male caregivers to your sessions, make the evening "Dads" and Children Only. Male caregivers will enjoy using new technology, such as Comic Life or Photostory, to create books, movies, and visual stories with their children. Creating secret messages, learning car games, and telling silly stories also have appeal for most dads. For more information on these and others workshops for dads, see *Getting Dads on Board* (Baskwill, 2009) pages 88–90.

Family Night Feedback

Dear Parents:

Please take a few minutes to complete this survey to let me know how you felt about our Family _____ Night. Your input will help me with planning the next event. Please return this form to me with your child.

Thank you.

If you are uncertain about a response, please circle 3: No Opinion	Strongly Disagree	Disagree	No Opinion	Agree	Strongly Agree
The activities were well organized.	1	2	3	4	5
The activities were interesting for the whole family.	1	2	3	4	5
I have a better understanding of the _____ curriculum.	1	2	3	4	5
I liked the format.	1	2	3	4	5
I would attend this event again.	1	2	3	4	5
There was enough help.	1	2	3	4	5

What station/activity did you like the best?

What suggestions do you have for me or what changes would you like to see to Family Nights?

Pembroke Publishers ©2013 *Attention-Grabbing Tools* by Jane Baskwill ISBN 978-1-55138-283-8

6

Take-Home Materials

My first book for teachers about working with parents, *Parents and Teachers: Partners in Learning* (Baskwill, 2009), featured a then-new idea: sending learning materials home. As a classroom teacher, it was my belief that communicating with parents required a variety of approaches, one of which was providing take-home materials.

I still firmly believe in this and have found over the years that when teachers offer a menu of ways parents can participate in their children's learning, they reach many more parents. The parent who never comes to school might be a faithful reader of the class newsletter or website; the parent who does not get out to many family nights might look forward to the next take-home activity.

Take-homes can be as elaborate as a self-contained learning package of materials and directions or as simple as a one-page Fridge Note on a particular topic. Both are tools for helping communicate to parents particular aspects of the curriculum and providing information about how they can help support their children's learning.

Take-Home Learning Kits

Take-home learning activities involve families in hands-on curriculum-related learning. They usually are self-contained packages of materials and directions provided by the teacher.

Some kits take the form of a regularly scheduled weekly take-home, such as Literacy Bags that contain picture books for parents to read aloud to their children. Some kits are sent home following a particular lesson or as an end-of-unit extension. When organized around a particular theme or curriculum topic, themed take-home kits offer great opportunities for parents and children to interact with the materials and to actively participate in the learning connection between home and school.

Learning kits provide opportunities for students and parents to get excited about learning they can do together. Here's how to create a take-home kit:

1. Create kits on a theme or specific curriculum topic. This will allow you to keep to a particular focus and find related materials. You will be creating only one or two versions of a specific kit, as it is not necessary to have a class set. The more variety the better.

2. Give each kit a creative name. You will grab the attention of parents and children alike with a name that will capture their curiosity and imagination: e.g., Spooky Science, Fairy Tale Math, Incredible Edibles, Creepy Crawlies.

3. Choose an easy-to-transport but durable storage container. Cloth bags or backpacks are popular, as are large self-closing plastic bags. However, you might find other unique totes: lunch boxes or bags, plastic storage boxes, cloth courier bags. Whatever you choose, make sure they hold all the materials you want to place inside and that they are easily portable. They should be eye-catching or able to be made so.

4. Assemble the materials you want to put inside the kits. Include a brief description of the kit and a list of materials contained inside. Choosing a book or poem to base your kit around makes things easy. Even if it is a science, math, social studies, or health kit, choosing one or more books on which to anchor the activities allows you to integrate your choices across the curriculum. If you can't find a book, or if funds are limited, poems are a viable option.

5. Label each kit with the name of the kit, information on where to return the kit should it be lost and found, and the number of the kit. If you number each kit, you will have an easy way to track the kits when you distribute them to families. A great way to label kits in containers that have handles is to use luggage tags from discount variety stores.

6. Prepare a letter introducing the kit to your students' families. Explain why you want to give them the opportunity to share this experience with their children and describe how the lending of the kits will work. If you send kits home for a week, include a weekend, rather than limiting the time to a Monday-to-Friday school week.

Board and card games make fantastic take-home kits for parents and children in the upper grades to enjoy together. For more information about developing and managing your kits see *Getting Dads on Board* (Baskwill, 2009) pages 91–95.

7. Get help in checking the kits. Ask for parent volunteers to come to school to help when the bags are returned. They can check the contents against the list in the kit and either replace what's missing from your supplies or make a note of what needs to be replaced. They can also be asked to make repairs as necessary.

When organized around a particular theme or curriculum topic, themed take-home kits offer great opportunities for parents and children to interact with the materials and to actively participate in the learning connection between home and school. Here are some examples:

- **I Dig Dinosaurs**: This kit is very popular for parents and children alike. Combine information about what paleontologists do with information about dinosaurs. Reader's Digest Pathfinders book *Dinosaurs* by Paul Willis and *Amazing Dinosaurs* by Dougal Dixon are two great choices for touchstone books for this kit. Include a bag of plastic dinosaurs for sorting or for use on a story mat or diorama; a magnifying glass and notebook for recording "finds"; and activities related to skeletons, such as matching a picture of an animal with its skeleton.
- **Wayfinding Kit:** The focus of this kit is maps. There are many books for children of all ages about using and making maps. A number of picture books show characters making and using maps, including *There's a Map on My Lap* by Tish Rabe; *The Once Upon a Time Map Book* by B.G. Hennessy; *Follow that Map! A First look at Mapping Skills* by Scot Ritchie. Include maps of your local area and province; map puzzles; directions for creating a map of the family's backyard or street where they live, or for creating a storybook map (e.g., Red Riding Hood's map to Grandma's). Also include a compass and directions for using it.

- **Measure Up:** Families have a lot of fun with this measurement kit. Great books from which to choose your touchstone book are *Actual Size* by Steve Jenkins; *Counting on Frank* by Rod Clement; *How Tall, How Short, How Far Away* by David Adler. Invite families to use a variety of tools, both standard and non-standard, to measure as many things as they can. You can generate a list of things to measure with your students in advance of putting this bag together. Among the tools, include a tape measure, a ruler, a stopwatch, string, snap-together cubes, paper clips, bingo chips, etc. Anything that is a uniform size can be used.
- **Feed Me!** Kids and cooking go hand-in-hand for this learning kit. A number of books will launch families into some creative cookery: *Cloudy With a Chance of Meatballs* by Judi and Ron Barrett; *Cook-A-Doodle Doo* by Janet Stevens and Susan Stevens Crummel; *The Everything Kids Cookbook* by Sandra Nissenberg; *Play with your Food* by Joost Elffers. Include a glossary of words commonly found in recipes; some easy-to-make recipes on cards (e.g., sandwiches, mac and cheese); blank recipe cards. A child-sized apron and measuring cups and spoons are nice additions.

LEARNING KIT IDEA: WEIRD AND WONDERFUL WEATHER

You will have no trouble finding books suitable for this themed kit: *Cloudy With A Chance of Meatballs* by Judi Barrett; *Weather Facts* by Usbourne; *Weather At Your Fingertips* by Judy Naylor; *Thunder Cake* by Patricia Polacco; *EyeWitness Weather* by Brian Cosgrove; *The Magic School Bus Inside a Hurricane* by Joanna Cole.

Materials and activities can include

- directions for making a Home Weather Station, along with a simple rain gauge, barometer, weather vane, and wind sock
- a Weather Journal and pages of basic weather information: types of clouds, weather words, online weather information sources, etc. Children can record weather information in the journal
- an inexpensive digital camera to take photos to be added to the Weather Journal
- a blank calendar for keeping track of the weather

Monthly Parenting Bags

This initiative is a little more costly and might require funding from your Parent/Teacher Association or from a local grant. However, it is another way to provide parents with positive support.

I began sending parenting books home when I was in the classroom, as I recognized that parents appreciate any help teachers can give them. Many are unsure about how to help their children with a number of issues, from learning to behavior. Those who feel more confident are still interested in parenting ideas and information. This project was first initiated with these parents in mind: see *Parents and Teachers: Partners in Learning* (Baskwill, 1989). Now that self-help books have become very popular as a go-to strategy for information about a host of topics, an initiative like this for parents remains timely. It offers parents a variety of self-help books on many aspects of child-raising.

To implement this activity, begin by collecting books you think parents would be interested in reading. Try to find books of a practical nature that include parenting tips and activities, along with some that focus on children's learning-support and behavior. Ask the librarian at your public library or staff at your local independent bookseller for a list of suggestions. Be sure to read as many of the books as possible—or, at the very least, skim them—to make sure the content is appropriate for your students' families.

Here are some things to keep in mind when creating and organizing parent bags:

- Find inexpensive sources of books. Many quality books can be found at flea markets and used bookstores, or can be acquired from other parents. Put out a call to the families in your school and you will be surprised how many excellent books for parents you will get.
- Schedule books to go home. Once a month is a good time frame. It allows parents ample time to read the book, should they wish. A tracking sheet (see page 73) can be added to your binder and will help you know which books families have.

SAMPLE MONTHLY TRACKING SHEET

Book	Oct	Nov	Dec	Jan	Feb	Mar	Apr	May
Becoming the Parent You Want to Be	Caplas	Frith	Olmath					
Chicken Soup for the Soul: Parenthood	Frith	Olmath	Caplas					
The Discipline Book	Olmath	Caplas	Frith					

- Label your bags well. Luggage tags work well on totes with handles.
- Include a brief description of the book. Write a paragraph or two in which you describe the book (similar to doing a book talk) and why you selected it. Mount the book description on card stock and laminate it, or put it in a page protector in a duotang folder. You can also put the information on a bookmark.

SAMPLE BOOK DESCRIPTION

> *Chicken Soup for the Soul: Parenthood*
> by Jack Canfield, Mark Victor Hazen, and Amy Newmark
>
> I know firsthand that parenting can be a tough job sometimes. This book will touch your heart and make you laugh as you read short stories and bits of advice from other parents about raising children of all ages.
>
> I thought this book would be a good choice to share with you. I look forward to hearing from you about what you think. Is there one story that stands out or is your favorite? Please let me know.

- Provide comment cards. In the back of each book put a large brown envelope or library pocket. Inside put an index card with the heading *What did you think?* After reading the book, write a brief comment about some part that you found helpful or interesting or especially enjoyed. Invite the parents to do likewise. You will find the comments revealing about how different books appeal to your students' families.
- Remember that there might be some families who are unable to read the books you provide. Offer the books to all families. Parents who cannot read the books

themselves might have a relative or friend with whom they can share the book. Or they can just hold on to it until the month is up. Don't pressure parents to read the books. Keep the invitation open and the selection varied. You might find that some books are available from the public library as audio books and can include information for parents about how they can be accessed.

- Introduce books to your students' families at your first Meet-the-Teacher or Curriculum Night in September.

Book bags for parents offer much more than a ready-made library coming into the home; they provide parents with another kind of support, one that offers them information in a nonthreatening way.

New books are coming out all the time. As well, there are a number of books that are considered classics. Highlight one of the books in the collection in your newsletter or on your website. The feedback you get from parents about the books, both in writing on the cards and in person, will help you know how each book is being received. Don't hesitate to retire a book that parents do not find useful.

Something to consider, especially if you are considering applying for funding to support your project, is purchasing several e-readers on which you can upload books for parents. Some have a read-aloud feature that will help parents who find reading difficult.

Books for Parent Bags

Becoming the Parent You Want to Be by Laura Davis and Janis Keyser (Three Rivers Press, 1997)

Chicken Soup for the Soul: Parenthood by Jack Canfield, Mark Victor Hazen, and Amy Newmark (Chicken Soup for the Soul, 2013)

The Discipline Book by William and Martha Sears (Little Brown & Company, 1995)

Help Your Kids with Math by Barry Lewis (Dorling Kindersley Ltd., 2010)

Help Your Kids with Science by Dorling Kindersley (Dorling Kindersley Ltd., 2012)

Helping Your Children with Reading and Writing at Home by Mary and William Colbert (Xlibris Corporation, 2009)

Hold Onto Your Kids by Gordon Neufield and Gabor Mate (Ballantine, 2006)

How to Talk so Kids Will Listen and How to Listen so Kids Will Talk by Adele Faber and Elaine Mazlish (Scribner, 2012)

Parenting from the Inside Out by Daniel Siegel and Mary Hartzell (Penguin, 2003)

Playful Parenting by Lawrence Cohen (Ballantine, 2002)

Positive Discipline by Jane Nelsen (Ballantine, 2006)

Respectful Parents, Respectful Kids by Sue Hart (Puddledancer Press, 2006)

Siblings Without Rivalry by Adele Faber and Elaine Mazlish (William Morrow, 2004)

Silly Books to Read Aloud by Rob Reid (Huron Street Press, 2013)

Unconditional Parenting by Alfie Kohn (Atria, 2006)

Fridge Notes

A Fridge Note is one or two pages of information for parents on a particular topic. Fridge Notes are meant to be hung on the refrigerator where parents can keep them for handy reference. They are concise and eye-catching reminders of information you have put in your newsletter or shared at a Family Night. They can also be sent in response to a question or topic of interest parents have been asking you about.

For instance, for parents of younger children, you might create a Fridge Note about:

- picture walks and how to do them
- a list of picture books for a specific purpose (i.e. imaginative play, science, math, class favorites, etc.)
- interactive drawing
- interactive reading tips
- how to support children's writing
- the importance of imaginative play with books that lend themselves to dramatic play

SAMPLE FRIDGE NOTE: PICTURE WALK

FRIDGE NOTE: Picture Walk

Conducting a picture walk before reading a story allows you to

- Create interest in reading the story and activate prior knowledge about the topic
- Learn about your child's understanding of his/her experience related to the story
- Help your child practice using visual cues (pictures) as a reading strategy
- Think about questions and concepts to explore with your child while reading

During the picture walk, talk about what you notice or wonder about, or what you think might happen next. Some useful questions/prompts to use include

- *Let's look at the front cover. What do you think this story is about?*
- *This is just like when you _____. An experience I had was...*
- *Turn the page. What do you see? What do you think is happening?*
- *What do you think will happen next?*
- *Here we are almost at the end of the book. How will the story end?*
- *What are you curious to know more about in the story? I wonder if...*

You and your child can take turns throughout the picture walk or you can each take a turn doing a whole picture walk yourself.

For parents of older children, send Fridge Notes about

- homework tips
- a list of URLs and book choices for a particular topic
- a scavenger hunt
- a science experiment with simple materials
- annotated reading lists
- directions for a family activity such as mapping

FRIDGE NOTE: Family Mapping Activity

When families write together they learn more about writing and more about each other. Here is a mapping activity for you to try at home that will motivate even the most reluctant writer!

Materials:
- Large sheets of paper
- Crayons, markers
- Personal journals or paper; writing implements

Here's what to do:

1. Talk about memories of things that happened at home or in your neighborhood growing up. Try having family members close their eyes and picture the community in which they grew up/are growing up. What does their house look like? The yard? The road? Who lives near them? What does their house look like? Are there churches? Stores?

2. Give everyone a piece of paper and ask them to draw a map of where they live/lived. Have them include as many details as they can—places, people's houses/names, etc.—that they think are important.

3. Together, share what is on each map and why it was put there.

4. Each person writes about a childhood experience that happened somewhere on their map. It sometimes helps to set a timer for ten minutes.

5. Share what you wrote.

I will be making space on our bulletin board if you want to send in some of your maps/memories to be posted there.

Fridge Notes are easy to create. When planning, look for opportunities where it would be useful for parents to have a ready reference. Keep a list for future reference. Some tips to creating your own Fridge Notes:

- Be brief. Try not to be too wordy. Use plain language and try not to cover too much on any one topic. You can always do a Part II later on.
- Make them eye-catching. Use decorative computer paper or graphics to capture your parents' attention. The page should stand out on the refrigerator.
- Use page protectors. Try to help your students get the Fridge Note home in good condition, as it is more likely to be put on the refrigerator that way. Insert the page in a page protector that is to be brought back to you to be used for the next one.

Fridge Notes can be easily incorporated into your classroom. Involve your students in composing the Fridge Note during a mini-lesson. It is a great way to demonstrate an authentic writing event.

- Discuss what a Fridge Note is and its purpose. Talk about the audience and the tone. Show students a sample by projecting it on your interactive whiteboard or screen.

- Talk with students about the decisions you made when composing the note and point out specific features; e.g., bulleted list, diagram. Point out ways in which you try to keep the reader's interest: e.g., attention-grabbing words, layout.
- Have students help you write a Fridge Note. Make it a simple one: e.g., an easy one to do together is listing the students' favorite fiction or nonfiction books. Together compose an opening paragraph about the content of the note, then follow with the list of books. You can keep the number of books to ten and vote for ones to put on the list, or you can list one from each student.
- Discuss how to make the note eye-catching: e.g., using clip art, photos, student drawings.

Fridge Notes are not meant to be a weekly take-home, and do not have to go home very often. They are to be used when there is a bit of information you would like to send home about supporting children's learning or when you have something you feel needs to be stressed or reviewed. Although they might contain a brief activity for parents to try, they are mainly condensed *how-tos* that describe a skill or strategy or that share information.

Books for Parent Bags: Monthly Tracking Sheet

Book	October	November	December	Jananuary	February	March	April	May

Pembroke Publishers ©2013 *Attention-Grabbing Tools* by Jane Baskwill ISBN 978-1-55138-283-8

7

Face-to-Face

The very best way to help parents gain an understanding of how their children are developing as learners is through conferencing. No report card can replace the sharing of information that takes place at a well-thought-out, face-to-face meeting. Too often, though, these meetings are reduced to a ten- to fifteen-minute whirlwind that follows assembly line precision, and time dictates what will be discussed. These meetings are unsatisfying for parent and teacher alike.

Some teachers have found ways to extend the obligatory school-wide meetings by scheduling more time or by adding after-school conferences. When alternatives to the sit-down conference are used, such as the use of Skype (see page 102), dialogue journals (see page 41), and special invitations or phone calls, hard-to-reach parents who might not come in for a conference are able to ask questions, receive information, and generally be kept up-to-date on their child's learning progress.

Parent–Teacher Conferences

Parent-teacher conferences extend communication between you and your students' parents. They give both parents and teacher a chance to sit down and share information about a child's learning. They are opportunities to keep parents informed about their child's learning progress and for collaborating on strategies that will ultimately benefit the child. While parent–teacher conferences are synonymous with report cards in the minds of many parents and teachers, they can be an effective tool for creating and maintaining the parent–teacher partnership at any time. Niva, a Grade 3 teacher, discovered that holding parent–teacher conferences before issues have built up can contribute to a positive relationship. She explained to me:

> I used to be so nervous about having a conference with a child's parents. It wasn't just the report-card conferences that I minded, it was any conference. I saw them as negative. As a result, I only met with parents when I had to and usually it wasn't very positive. Parents usually left upset and I felt miserable too. When I asked you for some suggestions, I didn't realize the solution was relatively simple. First of all, you suggested I consider having meetings with parents between the reporting periods. That way, any issues could be picked up as they happened and not after they piled up. Second, you gave me a planner. That made all the difference in the world for me. After preparing and writing down what I wanted to focus on, I felt much more confident and ready to really discuss the child's strengths and to ask parents for their help brainstorming how to support any areas of need. It was so obvious—be prepared. Thanks.

Although these suggestions refer to the report-card conference, most are appropriate any time you meet with a parent.

As Niva discovered, conferences need not just be at report-card time. If parents feel they are being kept informed, they will be willing to hear the successes as well as the challenges. Here are some important things to consider in order to make the parent–teacher conference a success.

IN ADVANCE

- Send home a letter with a special invitation for parents. Tell them what they can expect when they arrive: if they are early, where to wait; how long you will have together; what if they need more time; etc.

SAMPLE LETTER

Dear Parents,

It is report-card conference time again and I look forward to meeting with you about your child's progress. I am trying to find ways to make the most of our time together. Therefore, I thought I would send home these Frequently Asked Questions. Hopefully you will find them helpful.

If I am early, should I come into the classroom?

Please wait until I come out and get you. I will have a waiting area where there will be chairs for parents to sit in. While you wait, please have a look at the materials I have placed on the table. I have been able to find some hand-outs for parents on health and bike safety. Please help yourself.

How long do we have?

We will have 15 minutes for our conference. This isn't a lot of time but we can still pack a lot in. It is helpful if you make a list, in order of importance, of the things you wish to discuss or about which you have questions. I will do the same. This will help us stay on track and cover what is most important. Please make sure you have gone over the report card before you come.

What if we need more time?

Sometimes a matter will come up that requires more discussion. If more time is needed, we can schedule another meeting at a time and day that works for both of us.

What if I can't keep my appointment?

If something unexpected comes up and you are unable to keep your appointment, please call the school and leave a message (XXX-XXXX) or e-mail me at teacher@ednet.ca. I will get back to you so we can try to reschedule.

If my child is doing well, do you still need to see me?

By all means! These conferences are for all parents. It is important for parents to discuss their child's progress and to learn about what their interests are and how you can foster these.

Remember, your parent–teacher conference is on _____
_____ at _____.

Sincerely,

- Arrange the space. Get out from behind your desk, as staying behind your desk sends the message that there is a separation between you and the parent. Be sure to have enough chairs for everyone. Use a round table whenever possible. If you are using a rectangular table, sit near the end of the long side with the parent seated at the short side. This will put you close to parents with just the corner of the table between you, rather than the separation you get when you seat parents opposite you. It also makes it easier for you to show examples of children's work or point out something you have brought to share. If there are two parents or a parent has brought an advocate or an interpreter, seat that person opposite you at the same end of the table.
- Use adult-sized furniture. You want to make sure everyone is comfortable and to be considerate of those who might have back or knee issues. If you must use smaller-sized furniture, apologize up front and ask if the classroom furniture will be okay for them. Have an alternative at the ready if it is not. Make sure you sit on a chair that is the same height as the parent's chair.
- Prepare a master list on which you have the names of the parent(s) and the time of the appointment. Try to schedule appointments with five minutes between the end of one and the start of the next to allow parents to enter and exit.
- Review each child's file. Collect dated samples of each child's work, along with any assessments you have done. Organize your samples in three piles: work that shows evidence of strong understanding; work that can be categorized as being at grade level; and work that reflects confusions or shows difficulties. Look for patterns of consistent strength or weakness and note them on your conference planner. This process should provide a clear picture of how the student is developing and help you identify which samples will provide parents with the most information. Select a focus for your conference, as you will not have time to go over everything.

See page 85 for the Parent–Teacher Conference Planner form; page 86 for the Parent-Teacher Conference Summary form.

- Use the Parent–Teacher Conference Planner form on page 85 as you prepare. This will keep you on track on the day.
- Set up a waiting area outside your classroom. Have a few chairs for those who arrive early. Make some parent-appropriate reading materials available.

ON THE DAY

- Keep to your schedule. Don't run over time. If you have found it difficult in the past to bring a conference to a close, consider using a timer. Tell parents you are going to set the timer and that when it goes off you will have to end the conference. Also tell them you would be happy to schedule another meeting. Even if you have put this in your letter (see page 76), you should repeat it quickly in the conference to avoid any hurt feelings or confusion. Keeping a clock in view will also help you and your parents better gauge your time.
- Organize student files in the order of the appointments. Be sure to confirm with parents that they are indeed who you were expecting. It never looks good if you start talking about a particular child when you should be talking about another!
- Assume nothing. Living arrangements and family circumstances vary. Clarify who is at your meeting and how they wish to be addressed before you begin. This is especially important at a first meeting or if there is someone present you hadn't expected.

- Make notes. Use the form you used to review your students' files and record notes of your session. Provide paper and pen for your parents and invite them to take notes if they would like.
- Keep a box of tissues and a bowl of mints on the table.

Making Sure Conferences Go Smoothly

- Greet parents at the door with a friendly smile. Show them to their seats. Let parents know they can stop you at any time to ask questions or make comments.
- Begin and end your conferences on a positive note. For parents to stay involved, they have to feel that something is going right. No one wants to hear a steady barrage of negative comments—especially about their child.
- Listen attentively. Use active listening to let parents see you are really interested in what they have to say.
- Keep the focus on the child's learning. Even behavior issues can be related back to a child's learning. Parents will become defensive if they feel you are attacking their child or being judgmental. When behavior issues are perceived to be what is most important, it can result in the parent looking for other avenues of blame; e.g., another student or the teacher. When your concern about behavior is linked to a concern about a child's learning progress, parents will be more willing to listen.
- Respond honestly to questions. You will likely know the answer to most questions parents ask, but if you don't, say so. Tell them you will find out and get back to them. Tell parents when they should expect a response and arrange for how that should happen (by phone, e-mail, etc.).
- Avoid using "education speak." Use plain language and avoid jargon.
- Collaboratively develop learning goals and a plan of action. If need be, arrange a date for a follow-up meeting. Make sure you write the information down for the parent. You can prepare slips of paper to have ready for this purpose.
- Keep records of each conference. Record what was talked about and list any suggestions or agreements made. See the Parent–Teacher Conference Summary form on page 86.

There are times when a conference is needed quickly. These meetings can be called by the teacher or the parent. Here are some guidelines to keep in mind:

- Try to find out the reason for the request before the meeting. I have found it helpful to say, "Can you tell me in general what you would like to talk about, so I can bring any information I might need?" Don't get into a conversation about the issue. Wait until the meeting.
- Prepare carefully. Have the child's file with you in case you need to refer to it. Review your school's policy handbook if appropriate; have a copy to which you can refer if necessary.
- Ensure privacy and confidentiality. Parents need to trust that whatever they choose to share with you will remain confidential. However, also keep in mind that there are times when you might not be able to keep what they tell you to yourself; this is especially true in the case of suspected abuse.
- Stay professional. Don't be tempted to talk about other children, parents, or teachers or to lay blame elsewhere. Keep focused on the individual child and the topic at hand.

- Make sure you and the parents fully understand the problem. Use phrases like "Let me see if I understand this correctly…" or "Just so we are all on the same page, can you please tell me what you understand the problem to be?"
- Solicit suggestions from parents in addition to any specific instructions you might share.
- Develop follow-up suggestions together. Commit to a follow-up communication by phone, face-to-face, or by e-mail.
- Always try to end the conference on a positive note.

Student-Led Parent Conferences

Student-led parent conferences are becoming more popular with teachers who realize that the traditional conference leaves out the very person whose learning is being discussed—the student. Evita found that, if they were given a little preparation, five- to six-year-old children could share their learning with their parents:

> I am so excited. I had my first student-led conferences with the parents and children of my Primary class and, from the feedback I received, they loved it! I prepared the children for talking to their parents and for showing the work we collected in their portfolios. I even had them practice on their reading buddies from Grade 4, whose teacher helped her students know what to ask and how to respond to the younger ones. It was amazing. Those kids really knew a lot about how they learn best, their interests, and what the samples showed about their learning progress. I definitely plan on doing it again.

Students of all ages can learn how to conduct effective conferences. Student-led conferences provide opportunities for students to present their work to their parents in an organized way. It is a time for sharing, celebrating, and goal-setting. Proponents of student-led conferences say that the practice

- gives students the opportunity to demonstrate their learning and explain it in their own words
- empowers students to be more accountable for their own learning
- gives students a better understanding of their own progress
- helps parents support their child's achievement in ways that are more individually appropriate
- gives insight into parent–child and child–teacher interaction
- fosters a deeper partnership between parent, child, and teacher
- keeps the focus on student learning

See page 87 for the Student-Led Conference Letter.

As Evita discovered, the hallmark of an effective student-led conference is preparation, not just by helping students create an authentic collection of evidence of their own progress, but also by readying parents to become active participants rather than passive receptors—something most parents are not used to doing in a conference setting. To help with this, send home a letter or post a video, explaining what parents can expect of a student-led conference; see Student-Led Conference Letter on page 87. Of equal importance is preparing students for sharing their understanding with their parents.

Because both parents and children enjoy the process so much, turnout for student-led parent conferences is often higher than for teacher-led conferences.

Conference Formats

Student-led conferences can take one of several formats, depending on the teacher, the school, and the grade.

THE THREE-WAY CONFERENCE

In a three-way conference, the teacher meets with each family and is present through all aspects of a child's conference. There is also a brief period of time scheduled for parents and teacher to meet alone. The following is a typical agenda for the three-way conference:

1. Greeting by teacher

2. Student shares
   - Letter to parent: a letter about student's work in general during the term
   - Goals: goals student has set at the beginning of the term
   - Learning portfolio samples: work chosen by the student
   - "Things I've Learned" sheet: student self-reflection on his/her learning, summarizing the portfolio samples

3. Teacher elaborates on report card and various skills

4. Child steps outside room to write in journal, usually a reflection on the conference

5. Last ten minutes for teacher and parents to discuss personal matters if needed.

6. Closing:
   - Parents meet child outside room to read student's journal and praise him/her on journal activity
   - Student thanks the parents for coming to the conference

See page 82 for more on learning portfolios.

CONCURRENT/FOUR CORNERS CONFERENCE

An effective strategy for organizing is to use a "four corners" approach, creating a station in each of the four corners of the classroom. As families rotate clockwise around the room, they engage their child in a discussion about the topic or materials that are at each station. Here are some examples:

1. **Portfolio Sharing**: At this station, children share portfolios of the work they have collected in class. In advance, students have reflected on selected pieces of work chosen for the portfolio. At the conference, students lead their parents through the learning evidence documented in their portfolio. For very young children, you might want to use audio or video recording to help a child record comments in advance and then play them back for parents. Some teachers have their children create PowerPoint presentations to accompany the portfolio, and both are shared at the station. (For more on portfolios see page 82.)

2. **Conference with the Teacher**: Two Stars and a Wish is a strategy often applied to writing conferences. It is also an effective way to help students consider their strengths and set a future goal. When applied to student-led conferences, students identify two learning areas in which they have done well over the course of the term (two stars) and set one goal to work on over the next term (one wish).

See page 88 for the Two Stars and a Wish form.

In advance of the conference, students reflect on their overall work and behavior and record it in the two stars and one wish format (see page 88 for the Two Stars and a Wish form) to share with parents and teacher. Parents should be encouraged at this station to share what they think are strengths they see in their child's learning and strategies to help their child reach their goal, while you do likewise.

3. **Literacy in Action**: At this station, gather a variety of literacy activities from which students can demonstrate learning to parents. Some students might choose writing tasks, such as journal writing or writing poetry. Others would rather conduct a book talk or read aloud their favorite picture book or passage from a novel. Still others might engage their parents in a word-making activity or game of scrabble.

4. **Other Curriculum Areas**: Create a station where you feature the learning of one or more curriculum areas. The more interactive this station is, the better. Students can choose from a variety of activities demonstrating concepts that have been learned in class. They then demonstrate to their parents how to conduct an experiment, engage their parents in a curriculum-related game, or solve a learning puzzle. Math and science activities work especially well at this station.

Some additional things to keep in mind:

- Limit the number of stations (no more than four).
- Set a time limit for each.
- Ring a bell when time is up. Parents and children will then rotate to the next station.
- Keep the stations interactive.
- Make sure students are familiar with the activities prior to the conference.
- Provide a Station Checklist Bookmark to help parents and children stay on track; see page 89 for reproducible bookmarks.
- In class, following the student-led conference, have students complete the Post-Conference Student Reflection; see page 90 for the form.
- In order to obtain feedback from parents after the student-led conference, send home a brief reflection tool; see page 91 for Post-Conference Parent Reflection tool. This will help you with planning future conferences.

See page 89 for reproducible Station Checklist Bookmarks; page 90 for the Post-Conference Student Reflection form; page 91 for the Post-Conference Parent Reflection tool.

Stations are an effective way for children to share their learning progress in student-led parent conferences. They are highly motivating and engaging for both student and parent, and support your school or district's learning outcomes.

THE CLASS PORTFOLIO CELEBRATION

In this format the entire class (or half the class on each of two nights) presents their portfolios to their parents. Usually a larger space, such as the school library or gym, is required for this event. Here's how to plan a celebration of student portfolios:

1. Devote time at Meet-the-Teacher/Curriculum Night to explain the three-way conference procedure.

2. Send home a conference schedule and sign-up sheet.

3. Two or three weeks prior to conferences, have students send invitations/ reminders to parents.

4. Explain the conference agenda in a letter to parents.

5. One week before conferences, have students practice with buddies, other adults, and partners.

6. Send report cards home prior to conferences so that parents are aware of successes, concerns, and their child's achievement and effort.

7. Have parents fill out the Reflection form on page 91 while students complete the Student Reflection form on page 90.

8. Set up an area for coffee, tea, and treats.

Learning Portfolios

A learning portfolio is a systematic collection of student work and reflections that helps paint a picture of the whole child. More than just a container of student work, the portfolio is dynamic and meaningful for students, teacher, and parents, as it reflects the process of collecting, selecting, and reflecting upon learning.

Portfolios of student work are the hub around which the student-led conference revolves; they can also be used as part of the traditional parent–teacher conference format. Portfolios

- celebrate the student's growth
- document progress
- showcase a range of work
- provide an organized sharing tool
- nurture students' independence and foster positive self-image
- encourage goal-setting and reflection

It is important to start right away by explaining student-led parent conferences to the class and helping students understand the portfolio collection/reflection/sharing process. In this way, the entire portfolio process becomes part of the classroom routine and integrated into your teaching.

1. Explain to students that they will be keeping their work in portfolios and will be sharing this work with their parents at conference time.

2. Put together a demonstration portfolio in which you have organized a selection of artifacts, along with your comments and reflections on each. You don't need to have a full term's worth of work, just enough so students can see the types of things they might put in their own portfolios. Demonstrate ways to organize the artifacts using dividers, large envelopes, page protectors, a list of contents, etc. Be sure to have your students date all their work.

3. On the whiteboard or on chart paper, begin a list with your students of some of the items they can include:
   - Curriculum-based work samples
   - Drawings
   - Photos
   - Audio/video recordings
   - Self-evaluations/Peer evaluations
   - Reflections
   - Lists of interests and talents

4. Add to the list over the course of the year. It is important for the portfolio to be multidimensional and to contain a wide variety of artifacts, demonstrating a number of different learning processes.

5. Ensure that some class time (at least bi-weekly) is devoted to working on portfolios. It is important to ensure that the portfolio is continuous and ongoing, and shows development over time.

6. Help students develop appropriate criteria for evaluating their portfolio. You might consider criteria such as
- Organization/Neatness
- Visual appeal
- Evidence of growth
- Variety of artifacts
- Evidence of positive attitude toward learning
- Balance of process and product
- Evidence of trying something new
- Achievement of curriculum outcomes
- Evidence of self-understanding

Be sure to put criteria in kid-friendly language that is appropriate to the age of your students. Mini-lessons that focus on each criterion will ensure your students' understanding of the criteria and demonstrate how to achieve them.

Remember, the contents of the portfolio are dynamic and should change on an ongoing basis.

7. Spend time helping students reflect on their learning. It is through the process of reflection that students come to understand themselves as learners. Students can share their reflections in small groups, with a partner, or in a conference setting with you.

It is also important to prepare parents to interact with their child during the sharing of the portfolio at the student-led conference.

1. Inform parents about the portfolio process at a meeting or in a letter.

2. Invite parents to be part of the process by explaining, just as you do with your students, the importance of the portfolio and its purpose. Explain that, by having students create the portfolio and prepare for the conference, you are asking students to consider their learning strengths and challenges.

3. Provide parents with sample questions to use with their children; see page 92 for the Portfolio Sharing Letter with sample questions.

See page 92 for the Portfolio Sharing Letter; page 93 for the Parent Feedback Letter.

4. Provide an opportunity for parents to write a short letter to their children about their learning progress; see page 93 for the Parent Feedback Letter.

Whether you hold student-led conferences or stay with the parent-only conference format, the portfolio is a very important tool for demonstrating student learning in an organized and thoughtful way.

Scheduling Traditional and Student-Led Parent Conferences

How you schedule your parent conferences will depend on your school's schedule and how much flexibility you have within that. Some schools easily accommodate the traditional conference along with student-led conferences, while others maintain separate schedules, with student-led conferences occurring on their own days/nights. You will need to discuss this with your principal.

Type of Conference	Length and Frequency	Format
Traditional Conferences: Back to Back	20–30 minutes, 8/day × 4 days	Teacher meets individually with each student's parent(s). Teacher leads conference.
Three-Way Conferences	45–60 minutes, 8/day × 4 days	Teacher sits in on conference led by the student.
Concurrent Student-Led Conferences	60 minutes, 8/day × 4 days	• Four at a time • Four corners with teacher at station
Class Portfolio Celebration		• Half or whole class at once • Teacher roams

Online Resources

"Student-Led Parent Conferences: How They Work in My Primary Classroom"
Powerful Learning Practice
http://plpnetwork.com/2012/01/13/student-led-parent-conferences-how-they-work-in-my-primary-classroom/

Student-Led Conferences: webcast of conferences at Grades 3 & 6
http://resources.curriculum.org/secretariat/studentled/index.shtml

"Student-Led Conferences: Up Close and Personal" (from *Ground Magazine*)
http://www.wired-and-inspired.ca/resources/student-led/index.html

Parent–Teacher Conference Planner

Student's Name:	Date of Conference:
Student's Strengths	**Student's Needs**

Samples and Assessment Records
Give evidence of performance

Home Learning Practices
List questions you have regarding student's learning interests and activities at home.

Your Goals for Student	Parental Goals for Student
1.	1.
2.	2.
3.	3.

Suggestions and Recommendations

Date of Follow-up:

Pembroke Publishers ©2013 *Attention-Grabbing Tools* by Jane Baskwill ISBN 978-1-55138-283-8

Parent-Teacher Conference Summary

Student's Name:

Date of Conference:

Conference type: ☐ Telephone ☐ In person ☐ Home Visit

Initiated by: ☐ Parent ☐ Teacher ☐ Principal ☐ Other:

Present at Conference

Purpose of Conference

Summary of Discussion and Recommendations

Pembroke Publishers ©2013 *Attention-Grabbing Tools* by Jane Baskwill ISBN 978-1-55138-283-8

Student-Led Conference Letter

Dear Parents,

Next week you will have the opportunity to participate in a conference led by your child. These student-led conferences will take place in our classroom. Your scheduled conference time is attached. The conference should take approximately ___ minutes.

Here is what you can expect:

1. Your child will be in charge of the conference and has planned to share specific samples of his/her work with you. Your child has rehearsed the conference in a specific order. Please allow your child to follow the special plan.

2. You will be shown completed work, see demonstrations of skills, and be told about the class and your child's daily activities. Several children will be conducting conferences in the classroom at the same time. Please do not bring other children and kindly switch off your cell phone during the conference so that your child will stay focused on the task.

3. Please be encouraging and provide positive feedback as your child shares his/her work with you. Ask questions that will help and support your child, but please try not to take over the conference.

4. I will be in the classroom to help keep the conferences running smoothly. Your child will share his/her strengths, successes, best work, and favorite subjects and activities. Your child might suggest areas in which he/she may want to improve. Please try to help your child make a plan for reaching his/her goal.

If you have any questions or concerns, please contact me. We can also make an appointment to meet privately if there are additional things you wish to discuss. I look forward to seeing you next week.

Sincerely,

Pembroke Publishers ©2013 *Attention-Grabbing Tools* by Jane Baskwill ISBN 978-1-55138-283-8

Two Stars and a Wish

Name: Date:

This is an opportunity to reflect on your learning progress over the term and for your parents and me to share that with you. On this paper, write down your two stars and one wish. Stars are learning strengths you feel you have. The wish is a learning goal you want to set for yourself for the next term.

★   Star 1:

★   Star 2:

☺   Wish:

Comments from my parent(s):

Station Checklist Bookmarks

Station Checklist for Student-Led Conference

Be sure to go to each of the 4 stations listed on this bookmark. Check each station off when you are done.

Remember to tidy the station materials before leaving.

A bell will tell you when it is time to change.

Parents, please leave a comment on the back of this bookmark about how your child's conference went and leave it in the container by the door.

☐ Portfolio Sharing: Share your portfolio and your reflections on your work.
☐ Conference with the Teacher: Share your Two Stars and a Wish list.
☐ Literacy in Action: Choose a writing or reading activity to share.
☐ Other Curriculum Areas: Share a math or science activity.

Thank you for coming!

Station Checklist for Student-Led Conference

Be sure to go to each of the 4 stations listed on this bookmark. Check each station off when you are done.

Remember to tidy the station materials before leaving.

A bell will tell you when it is time to change.

Parents, please leave a comment on the back of this bookmark about how your child's conference went and leave it in the container by the door.

☐ Portfolio Sharing: Share your portfolio and your reflections on your work.
☐ Conference with the Teacher: Share your Two Stars and a Wish list.
☐ Literacy in Action: Choose a writing or reading activity to share.
☐ Other Curriculum Areas: Share a math or science activity.

Thank you for coming!

Station Checklist for Student-Led Conference

Be sure to go to each of the 4 stations listed on this bookmark. Check each station off when you are done.

Remember to tidy the station materials before leaving.

A bell will tell you when it is time to change.

Parents, please leave a comment on the back of this bookmark about how your child's conference went and leave it in the container by the door.

☐ Portfolio Sharing: Share your portfolio and your reflections on your work.
☐ Conference with the Teacher: Share your Two Stars and a Wish list.
☐ Literacy in Action: Choose a writing or reading activity to share.
☐ Other Curriculum Areas: Share a math or science activity.

Thank you for coming!

Station Checklist for Student-Led Conference

Be sure to go to each of the 4 stations listed on this bookmark. Check each station off when you are done.

Remember to tidy the station materials before leaving.

A bell will tell you when it is time to change.

Parents, please leave a comment on the back of this bookmark about how your child's conference went and leave it in the container by the door.

☐ Portfolio Sharing: Share your portfolio and your reflections on your work.
☐ Conference with the Teacher: Share your Two Stars and a Wish list.
☐ Literacy in Action: Choose a writing or reading activity to share.
☐ Other Curriculum Areas: Share a math or science activity.

Thank you for coming!

Station Checklist for Student-Led Conference

Be sure to go to each of the 4 stations listed on this bookmark. Check each station off when you are done.

Remember to tidy the station materials before leaving.

A bell will tell you when it is time to change.

Parents, please leave a comment on the back of this bookmark about how your child's conference went and leave it in the container by the door.

☐ Portfolio Sharing: Share your portfolio and your reflections on your work.
☐ Conference with the Teacher: Share your Two Stars and a Wish list.
☐ Literacy in Action: Choose a writing or reading activity to share.
☐ Other Curriculum Areas: Share a math or science activity.

Thank you for coming!

Pembroke Publishers ©2013 *Attention-Grabbing Tools* by Jane Baskwill ISBN 978-1-55138-283-8

Post-Conference Student Reflection

Name: Date:

The best part of my conference was

During my conference, I think my parents learned

Next time when I do my conference, I will

Pembroke Publishers ©2013 *Attention-Grabbing Tools* by Jane Baskwill ISBN 978-1-55138-283-8

Post-Conference Parent Reflection

Student's Name: Date:

Dear Parents,

Thank you for taking such an active role in your child's conference. Please take a moment to answer the following questions. Your feedback is important to me and will help me plan for our next student-led conference.

What is something you learned about your child during the conference?

In what areas has your child demonstrated growth through his/her conference?

What suggestions/comments do you have?

Pembroke Publishers ©2013 *Attention-Grabbing Tools* by Jane Baskwill ISBN 978-1-55138-283-8

Portfolio Sharing Letter

Dear Parents:

The student-led conference is meant to be a conversation between your child and you about his/her learning progress. Here are some questions you might ask during the conference. Please feel free to ask questions of your own. Remember, this is a time to find out about your child's learning progress and to be supportive of their future learning goals.

What are some of the things you like to do in school?

What do you think you do well?

What has been the hardest thing to learn this term?

Is there any way your parents or teacher can help you learn better?

What helps you learn best when you are at home?

What helps you learn best when you are at school?

How do you get along with the others in your class?

Who are your friends?

Are you having any problems with anyone that we should talk about?

What is the goal you have set for yourself this term? How can we help?

Let's talk about homework. What is your favorite homework activity? How can we help you with your homework?

Pembroke Publishers ©2013 *Attention-Grabbing Tools* by Jane Baskwill ISBN 978-1-55138-283-8

Parent Feedback Letter

Dear Parent:

The main purposes for portfolios are to celebrate growth, to encourage students to think about their learning progress, and to help them learn to set goals. Your child's portfolio is a collection of work that shows the variety of work your child is doing, what your child feels he/she is doing well, and what your child wants to improve upon. Each piece has been carefully chosen to be shared with you. After your child has finished sharing his/her portfolio, please write a letter to your child, showing your support and encouragement.

Dear _____,

8

Communication in the Digital Age

Today's teachers are increasingly turning to a variety of digital technologies to make communication with parents easier and more current. As you consider what platform you will use to deliver information and communicate with parents (see page 10), keep in mind that not all parents have access to (or feel comfortable with) new technology. This might be the case for you as well. The good thing is that you do not have to go it alone.

- Learn alongside your parents. Explain to parents that this is a new venture for you, too. Parents will feel more at ease, knowing the teacher is experiencing the same challenges. Invite parents with expertise to help. Often, among your parents, there will be someone with an interest or skill with the new media you wish to implement. Ask if they are willing to help, should you need it.
- Seek out colleagues. If you explain to colleagues what you are trying to do, they might want to try it too. Others might already have some experience using the technology you are about to try and may be willing to mentor you.
- Use professional development (PD) opportunities. Consider creating a learning goal for yourself that focuses on using new technology with parents as part of your district professional development process. Another option is to try to get it on the agenda for your Professional Learning Community (PLC) if your school or district has this PD option.

As with anything new you take on, it can take some time before you have a good grasp of the digital media in which you are interested. As you experiment with each tool, you will gain a better understanding of how each works and what works best for you and your students' parents.

Webpages and Blogs

Two of the most popular and widely used tools are webpages and blogs. Keep in mind that each tool is designed to work differently, so it is important for you to decide which will work best for you. It is important to consider the time you have to spend on maintaining your webpage or blog. Parents will easily lose interest if you don't maintain your site.

There are some basic differences between webpages and blogs.

Teacher Webpage	Blog
Non-interactive	Interactive, allowing for the posting of comments after each post

Teacher Webpage	Blog
One-way communication	Social-media sharing options (i.e., Facebook, Twitter, etc)
Content created by teacher (some include classroom photos and samples of student work)	Content created by individual teachers or groups (parents and students in the teacher's class)
Static: tend to be updated infrequently (once or twice a year at end of term)	Updated frequently (weekly or even daily)
Collection of information for parents	Parents become partners in the education of their children through interaction with the thoughts and ideas the teacher posts for consideration or discussion

Webpages

Many schools and districts require their teachers to have a class webpage that is accessed through a link on the school website. Many teachers are more comfortable with this medium than with a more public space for conversations with parents about school or their classroom. The most successful webpages stay current, with information changing monthly or even more often.

Having a classroom webpage is a good way to connect school and home. In addition to the classroom site, some teachers give each child in the class his or her own page to which to submit items for posting. Both students and parents are excited to see students' classwork online.

The class website can contain your newsletter, information about class rules and homework policy, and photos of the classroom in action, as well as information about what the students are working on in the various curriculum areas. Links to sites that will be of interest to parents and children are a great addition. You can also set up the class webpage with a guest book. This is a great way to receive parent and family feedback.

It is important for your webpage to be designed well. Most user-friendly webpage creation tools are set up to use good web design principles for the following aspects:

TEXT

- Background is not showy or "in your face."
- Text size is big enough to read, but not too big.
- Headings highlight topics or sections.
- Columns of text are narrower than in a book, to make reading easier on the screen.

NAVIGATION

- Navigation buttons and bars are easy to understand and use.
- Navigation is consistent throughout website.
- Navigation buttons and bars provide the visitor with a clue as to where in the site they are.
- A large site usually has an index or site map.

- Buttons and graphics are tasteful, not too big or gimmicky.

GENERAL DESIGN
- Pages download quickly.
- Good use of graphic elements (photos, subheads, pull quotes) breaks up large areas of text.
- Every webpage in the site looks like it belongs to the same site; there are common elements that carry throughout the pages.

You should keep these principles in mind when doing your own web design or when choosing a webpage creation tool.

Online Resources

These days it is very easy for anyone to create an eye-catching webpage. There are free programs on the Internet that will take you through the process in a few easy steps. You want to make sure they also offer free hosting. At www.weebly.com, for example, you can create an attractive website and for no cost have it fully functioning in just a few hours.

Blogs

Blogs are powerful communication tools. When well done, they are opportunities for teachers to read, think, and reflect, connecting their students' learning to their classroom practice. Two good reasons for teachers to keep a blog:

1. *A blog attracts parents' attention.* Having a blog that talks about teaching and learning, with the aim of sharing knowledge with parents, is a great way for you to help parents deal with issues that affect their children and to support them by helping them support their children's learning. Following your blog might lead to a parent becoming more involved, based on something they have read that inspires them.

2. *A blog lets parents see that teachers are people.* Parents appreciate getting to know their child's teacher as a person. It helps to build rapport and establish a closer relationship. Of course, there is a danger of being too personal, so be sure to keep blog posts and photos related to your professional life. If you go on a trip, you can post pictures of the countryside and talk about what you have learned about the area, but no swimsuit or bar photos! Going to a summer workshop or taking a course are great things to blog about, as are posts about books you have read.

Online Resources

It is now easier than ever to create a blog. Some user-friendly sites that can help you create your blog:
www.weebly.com
http://edublogs.org/
http://wordpress.com/
http://googleblog.blogspot.ca/

Have a look at some of the blogs on the sites listed in the box, or look at some of your favorites from Internet searches, to see what style appeals to you and the type of content found there. You want to select a site that allows you to put up new content easily; anything that requires too many steps is not likely to remain current because of your busy schedule.

As with any type of writing, you will want to find your own voice. Blogs can be general in nature, focusing on your teaching and your students' learning; or they can be devoted to a specific topic such as math, science, nutrition and physical activity, etc.

SAMPLE BLOG SCREENSHOT

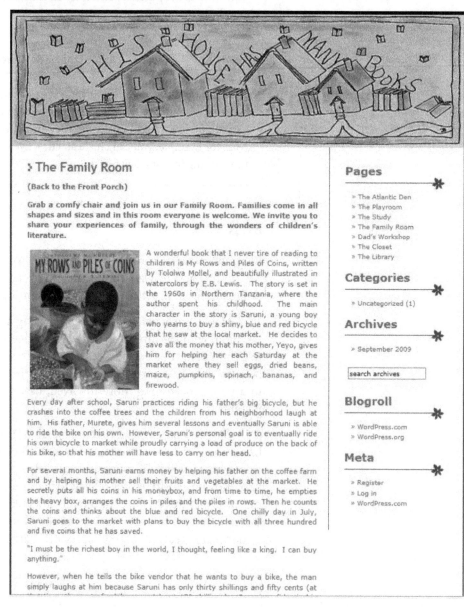

Regardless of the focus of your blog, here are the steps you can take to get it going:

1. Find your voice. Stay away from too much jargon and keep the tone friendly and upbeat.

2. Make a commitment. Remember that you must be willing to make a time commitment to maintaining your blog and to see it through once you begin.

3. Seek help. Talk to a colleague or friend who is a blogger and seek out helpful tips. There are a number of websites with tips for blog writing. A very helpful one can be found on the *Teaching English* website at http://www.teachingenglish.org.uk/help/how-to-write-a-good-blog

4. Be mindful of school policies. School districts have guidelines and acceptable-use policies (AUP) regarding the use of school- and division-wide computer networks and the Internet. These terms and conditions identify acceptable online behavior and access privileges. Policies regarding the use of photos and the display of student work must be adhered to strictly. Be sure to check into your district's policies.

E-Mail

E-mail has made communication with parents much easier. Many parents have e-mail accounts that they can access from home, work, or community sites. Teachers no longer need to worry about sending notes home with children or trying to reach a busy parent by phone. Parents are able to receive messages while working and are able to respond at a time that suits their schedule.

While e-mail is easy to use, it is also easy to misuse. Just as with any communication method, it is important to keep all communication with parents professional. Here are some things to keep in mind:

- Smilies (emoticons) or text message abbreviations can seem cute or friendly but might result in making it difficult to get your point across. Too much informality can be read as being disrespectful.
- Think about the implied tone of your message, especially when e-mailing about a behavior issue, as it is easy for parents to misinterpret the tone as being harsher than you intend. When in doubt, have a colleague read your e-mail to consider how it might be received.
- E-mails should not be used for communicating about serious issues. A meeting is usually best for this. However, e-mails can be useful for setting up meetings, sending positive notes of praise, reminding parents about an upcoming project or event, or sharing a minor concern.
- Send home the Parent Contact Information Survey (page 24) at the beginning of the school year to determine who is interested in having you communicate in this way.
- Be sure to follow through. Parents who opt to have messages sent to them will appreciate that you actually contact them by e-mail at least monthly, if not more often.

Social-Media Tools

Increasingly, social-media tools, such as Facebook and Twitter, are helping teachers keep parents and other community members informed. Teachers are encouraged to go where the parents are; more parents are apt to be on Facebook or

Twitter every day, whereas they might check the class webpage only once in a while or when reminded.

Facebook

Since many parents are already on Facebook, it makes sense to communicate with them on a platform with which they are already familiar, one that is already part of their daily routine. As the use of Facebook continues to grow, more and more issues arise regarding its use. Although some teachers remain unsure about whether or not to have a Facebook profile, others see it as a new opportunity for communicating with parents.

Facebook allows you to share class news and information with the parents of your students. You can create a parents' group for your class and share information only with the parents of your students. Some types of information you might share: details of upcoming field trips; school closings (scheduled or unforeseen); special events or parties; pictures of student projects; students' published writing; etc.

If you are considering using Facebook, it is important to be informed about policies or guidelines concerning its use that might be set out by your school district. For some teachers, Facebook will be strictly off-limits. However, if your district permits teachers to use Facebook for communicating with parents, there are some things you should keep in mind:

- Be professional. Maintain the same personal boundaries that you have with parents in the classroom setting.
- Your classroom Facebook page should relate only to your classroom. Nothing should be on the page that you would not proudly share with your principal or superintendent.
- Keep the focus on teaching and learning. The page you create should be a digital representation of your class and curriculum, and be a place where you encourage feedback.
- When you set up your page, use more than just your first and last name. Be sure to include the name of your class; e.g., Mrs. Macintosh's Grade 4 Class.
- Use a picture of your class mascot or a favorite image (perhaps a child's drawing of you) as your profile picture to keep the page geared to the classroom and curriculum. It should not be a picture from your personal life unless it relates to your classroom; for example, a picture of you reading a new children's book is fine.
- Include your Facebook address in your first letter home to parents and explain what you will use the forum for. Be clear and explicit so parents will understand your reasons for having a variety of ways by which you will communicate with them.

Facebook has a feature that allows you to post updates that parents will see immediately when they log onto their page. You can post information that pertains to homework—for example, "Don't forget that the Science Fair project is due on Wednesday"—to clarify a new policy, or to detail directions for an assignment. Parents can also send you a private message to ask questions about homework or to ask for a meeting. Parents who might be uncomfortable asking questions in person might feel more at home when using this medium.

Twitter

Twitter is another platform with which many parents have experience—or are eager to learn about. Twitter is a communication tool in which information is communicated in short posts of up to 140 characters (called Tweets). It is also possible to post links, photos, and videos.

Just as with Facebook, it is possible to set up your Twitter account so that only approved followers can view your Tweets. Tweets are most often sent using a smartphone, but can also be sent via computer. Twitter can be used to

- post reminders about events
- share news of the day
- share photographs and information from school-wide activities and class trips

Teachers of young children can use Twitter to let a parent of an upset or nervous child know how that child is doing. With children who are on a behavior plan, building Twitter into the plan can let the child know that the parent and teacher are on the same page. A Grade 5 teacher who uses Twitter has designated one of the jobs in her classroom as that of Tweeter. The student with this job Tweets two or three times a day about classroom learning activities; sometimes a photo is included (the student also has Photographer as a class job).

Teachers using Twitter find they can contact parents quickly if a child is sick or can keep parents informed of an activity they might do with their family to extend their child's learning in a particular curriculum area. When new children's books come out, a Grade 2 teacher I know Tweets about them. A Grade 6 teacher I met started using Twitter to see if more parents would attend his parent–teacher conferences if he reminded parents of them the morning of the conference. You might consider having a session for parents to help them set up their Twitter accounts.

Not every parent will want to use Twitter. It is not designed to replace e-mail communication, which can be more expressive, or the class webpage, which gives much more detail. It is just one more communication tool worth investigating to add to your toolkit.

Online Surveys

Surveys are excellent tools for gathering information from parents. They allow you to find out the best date and time for an event or meeting; how parents prefer to be contacted; whether they feel the homework given is too little, too much, or just right.

Keep in mind that, although you might have parents who prefer an online survey, you will also need to send home a paper version for those who don't. Make sure you find out how parents wish to respond in your first questionnaire at the beginning of the year.

There might be no limit to the number of questions you can ask on a survey; however, just as with a paper survey, it is best to keep the number of questions between eight and ten. Usually there is no limit to the number of participants you can have. Some survey-creator tools, such as Smart-survey, allow you to offer questions in different languages. After the online survey is completed by your students' parents, the survey-creator tool usually calculates and displays the results.

Online survey creators are simple and user-friendly. Many offer ready-to-use professional templates to make survey creation easy. They also feature a number of other benefits.

SAMPLE ONLINE SURVEY CREATOR

Permission for screenshot granted by SurveyMonkey

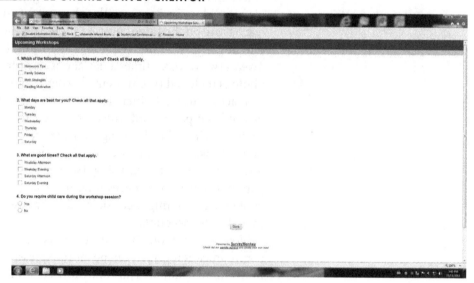

Internet Phone

You can download Skype for free at http://www.skype.com/intl/en-us/get-skype/

Software applications like Skype provide a way to talk to people over the Internet for free using a web cam and microphone. Calls can be audio only or include video. It is an excellent way to communicate with parents whose jobs or schedules do not permit them to communicate with you in person. Teachers I have spoken with have used it with parents who

- are in the military and are posted out of the province or overseas
- have work hours that are hard to schedule around
- have childcare, transportation, or personal-health needs

Video conferencing allows these parents to take part in the conference, feel involved, and even see some of their child's work.

Virtual Pinboards

Platforms like Pinterest support a virtual pinboard that allows users to pin images from blogs and websites, making them easier to refer to later. Virtual pinboards are visually appealing and easy-to-use. You can use this tool to set up boards that will be of interest to your parents and students. Create boards that you think would interest your parents:

- Arts and Crafts
- Books and Activities
- Nutrition and Recipes
- For and About Parents
- Places to Go, Things to See
- Kids and the Environment
- Math and Science Activities

You can add boards and change content as you wish. For example, if it is Science Fair time, you might have a board dedicated to science activities and experiments; you can devote a board to a particular social studies topic. Make parents aware of your site and how to set up an account so they can access it.

Once they have a account of their own, they can follow you and add content to their site by *repinning* the ideas and activities they see and like or by *pinning* ones they find on their own.

Pinterest is a lot of fun to use and is very easy for both you and your students' parents. Starting parents off with something that is practical, enjoyable, and easy-to-use is a great way to initiate them into using technology. Once parents are successful with Pinterest, they might be more open to exploring your website, using e-mail, or commenting on your blog.

Regardless of whether you use some or none of these tools, try to keep abreast of what is out there. You might hit upon just the right way to communicate with your parents and make parent-teacher communication a truly interactive experience for you both.

Concluding Thoughts

More and more, teachers and administrators are realizing the need to find creative and varied approaches to involve parents in their children's learning throughout the grades. Conferences and workshops for parents, displays of children's work in public places, and celebrations of children's learning and talents, along with a host of communication tools, are all designed to demonstrate what children are learning and provide a menu of communication options to reach most parents.

If I have learned anything in my years of teaching and working with parents, it's that, if parents are to become actively involved in their child's learning in positive and supportive ways, they must understand what is going on and know they have a rightful place in their child's education. Parents can be a powerful support group. It is important that teachers provide fair and sound teaching practices and develop communication methods that convey this message to parents and engage their support.

Parents are more concerned than ever that their children are receiving the best possible education. When they look at the work their children bring home and find they are unable to help, it scares them. It is important that teachers, administrators, and school districts keep things from reaching the stage where parents react negatively or give up because they feel nothing can be done. Parents' confidence and trust must be built slowly and carefully. Parents' feeling that they do have a place in the education of their children must be fostered and maintained, along with the feeling that their support and involvement will make a difference.

As teachers, we must be sure that we do not underestimate the capabilities of parents. We must make ourselves clear and be sure we listen to the wants and needs of the parents of our students.

It is very important to take stock of the communication methods we are currently using and explore all the other tools we might use. This is a very exciting time in the area of parental involvement and communication. There are far more options for engaging parents as partners in their children's education now than ever before. Some options will appeal to one group of parents, while others will appeal to another. Try to use a wide variety. Keep your communication interesting and current; above all, make certain you see the value in the communication tools you choose.

Teachers who see parents as partners in a child's learning journey will see communication with them as a two-way street; they will provide a variety of options for achieving this and keeping the communication going. Ultimately, it is the child who benefits, which is, after all, why we teach!

Resources

Baskwill, J. (1989) *Parents and Teachers: Partners in Learning.* Toronto, ON: Scholastic.

Baskwill, J. (2009) *Getting Dads on Board.* Markham, ON: Pembroke.

Baskwill, J. (2010) *Books as Bridges* Markham, ON: Pembroke.

Epstein, J. (2001) *School, Family, and Community Partnerships.* Boulder, CO: Westview.

Fleming, B.A. (1993) "From Visitors to Partners: A summary of effective parent involvement practices" in Rebecca Crawford Burns (Ed.), *Parents and Schools: From Visitors to Partners*, 77–89. Washington, DC: National Education Association.

Henderson, A.T., & Berla, N. (1997) *A New Generation of Evidence: The family is critical to student achievement.* Washington, DC: National Committee for Citizens in Education.

Henderson, A., & Mapp, K. (2002) *A New Wave of Evidence: The impact of school, family, and community connections on student achievement.* Austin, TX: Southwest Educational Development Laboratory.

Henderson, A.T., Johnson, V., Mapp, K.L., & Davies, D. (2007) *Beyond the Bake Sale: The essential guide to family/school partnerships.* New York, NY: New Press.

Howe, F. & Simmons, B.J. (1993) *Nurturing the Parent Teacher Alliance: A guide to forming a facilitative relationship.* ERIC Document Reproduction Service No. ED 358 086.

Lopez, G.R. (2001) "On Whose Terms? Understanding involvement through the eyes of migrant parents" Paper presented at the Annual Meeting of the American Educational Research Association, Seattle, WA.

Mapp, K.L. (2003) "Having Their Say: Parents describe why and how they are engaged in their children's learning" *The School-Community Journal*, 13(1), 35–64.

Patrikakou, E.N., Weissberg, R., Redding, S., and Walberg, H.J. (2005) *School-Family Partnerships for Children's Success.* New York, NY: Columbia University Press.

Science

Heil, D. (1999) *Family Science.* Portland, OR: Portland State University.

Hogue, L. (2000) *Science Night: Family Fun From A-Z.* Cincinnati, OH: Terrific Science Press.

Markle, S. (2005) *Family Science: Activities, Projects, and Games that Get Everyone Excited about Science!* Mississauga, ON: John Wiley & Sons.

Math

Kerr, J. (1986) *Family Math.* Berkeley, CA: Lawrence Hall of Science.

Diller, D. (2011) *Math Work Stations.* Portland, ME: Stenhouse.

Wedekind, K.O. (2011) *Math Exchanges.* Portland, ME: Stenhouse.

Whitin, D. & Wilde, S. (1992) *Read Any Good Math Lately?* Portsmouth, NJ: Heinemann.

Literacy

Anderson, J. (2011) *10 Things Every Writer Needs to Know.* Portland, ME: Stenhouse.

Booth, D. (2006) *Reading Doesn't Matter Anymore… Shattering the Myths of Literacy.* Markham, ON: Pembroke.

Dorfman, L. & Cappelli, R. (2012) *Poetry Mentor Texts: Making reading and writing connections, K–8.* Portland, ME: Stenhouse.

Dorfman, L. & Cappelli, R. (2007) *Mentor Texts: Teaching writing through children's literature.* Portland, ME: Stenhouse.

Foster, G. (2005) *What Good Readers Do.* Markham, ON: Pembroke.

Foster, G. (2012) *Ban the Book Report: Promoting frequent and enthusiastic reading.* Markham, ON: Pembroke.

Harvey, S. & Goudvis, A. (2007) *Strategies That Work: Teaching comprehension for understanding and engagement.* Portland, ME: Stenhouse.

Hindley, J. (1996). *In the Company of Children.* Portland, ME: Stenhouse.

Hutchins, D. (2007) *Family Reading Night.* Larchmont, NY: Eye On Education.

Johnson, P. (2000) *Making Books.* Markham, ON: Pembroke.

Johnson, P. & Keier, K. (2010) *Catching Readers Before They Fall: Supporting readers who struggle.* Portland, ME: Stenhouse.

Parsons, L. (2001) *Response Journals Revisited.* Markham, ON: Pembroke.

Peterson, S. & Schwartz, L. (2008) *Good Books Matter.* Markham, ON: Pembroke.

Rowsell, J. (2006) *Family Literacy Experiences: Creating reading and writing opportunities that support classroom learning.* Markham, ON: Pembroke.

Stead, T. (2008) *Good Choice! Supporting reading and response.* Portland, ME: Stenhouse.

Especially for Parents

Butler, D. & Clay, M. (2008) *Reading Begins at Home.* Portsmouth, NJ: Heinemann.

Hill, B.C. (2007) *Supporting Your Child's Literacy Learning: A guide for parents.* Portsmouth, NJ: Heinemann.

Clay, M. (1987) *Writing Begins at Home.* Portsmouth, NJ: Heinemann.

Clay, M. (2010) *How Very Young Children Explore Writing.* Portsmouth, NJ: Heinemann.

Clay, M. (2010) *The Puzzling Code.* Portsmouth, NJ: Heinemann.

Clay, M. (2010) *What Changes in Writing Can I See?* Portsmouth, NJ: Heinemann.

Websites

ABC Canada, Family Literacy Day information
http://abclifeliteracy.ca/fld/family-literacy-day

Harvard Family Research Project hosts FINE, a network of educators, practitioners, policymakers, and researchers dedicated to strengthening family–school–community partnerships.
http://www.hfrp.org/family-involvement/fine-family-involvement-network-of-educators

National Literacy Trust in the UK provides information and resources for working with parents.
http://www.literacytrust.org.uk/

People for Education has a number of resources related to parent involvement in education. Although aimed at parents, the information is pertinent for teachers, and includes links to other useful sites.
http://www.peopleforeducation.ca/global-topic/parent-involvement/view_type/document/

Reading Rockets pairs fiction and nonfiction books on a theme and has *Adventure Pack* materials for free download. For K–3, but can be adapted for higher grades.
http://www.readingrockets.org/article/27935/

Index